How to Write a Rest .... Steps
2019 Business Plan .... mplate Included

Table of Contents

Acknowledgments...4

About the Author 5

Introduction 6

Step 1 – Restaurant Description 8

Restaurant Summary:...8

Competitive Advantages: 9

Product / Service Description: 10

Pricing Strategy: 11

Business Models:..13

Location: 15

Future Plans: 16

Business Objectives and Time Line:................................17

Mission Statement: 19

Vision Statement:...19

Value Statement:..20

Keys to Success:...21

Step 2 – Target Market..24

Primary Target Market: 24

Secondary Target Market: 26

Target Market Growth Potential:....................................26

Step 3– Market Analysis 28

Industry Overview:...28

Industry Statistics: 29

Threats, Trends, and Opportunities: 30

Keys to Success: 31

SWOT Analysis: 32

Competitive Analysis: 34

Step 4 – Organization and Management 36

Management Summary: 36

Job Responsibilities: 37

Step 5 – Organizational Chart 39

Organizational Chart: 39

Step 6 – Marketing 42

Marketing Objectives and Keys to Success: 42

Traditional Marketing: 43

Internet Marketing: 44

Social Media Marketing: 45

Step 7 – Financials 47

Financial Assumptions: 47

Financial Summary: 49

Startup/Expansion Costs: 50

Daily Revenues: 52

Labor: 54

Monthly Fixed Costs: 55

Growth Rates: 56

Misc. Information: 57

Loan Payment Calculation: 57

Profit and Loss for 12 Months: 58

Income Statement: 61

Balance Sheet:...64

Financial Ratios: 67

Step 8 – Funding Request **71**

Potential Funding Sources: 72

Funding Terms:..73

Use of Funds:..74

Fund Repayment: 75

Step 9 – Executive Summary.......................................**77**

Restaurant and Product:...77

Target Market: 78

Financial Highlights:..79

Funding: 80

Step 10 – Appendix..**81**

Resumes:...81

Summary..**85**

Restaurant Business Plan Sample **86**

Restaurant Business Plan Template (Includes Market Research!)
....**117**

Acknowledgments

The drive and determination to write this short novel was in no small part due to my wonderful wife, Tishauna, kids, Cara, Katy, Maggie, and Paul Jr., stepson, Jayden and parents.

About the Author

Paul Borosky, MBA., Doctoral Candidate, is the owner of Quality Business Plan, Tutor4Finance, World Traveler Updates and FinanceHomeworkHelp.net. His time is mostly spent with his family, business plan writing, writing books, financial modeling and cruising. Oh, so many cruises.

Paul's first run-in with finance was as a mortgage broker in the mid-1990s. His fascination with finance led to an MBA with numerous credits in different finance courses. Recently, he has created two finance curriculums for a local college and is considered a subject matter expert in finance.

Currently, Paul is completing his dissertation, writing business plans, tutoring finance to students the world-over and teaching finance for a local college. In the future, he intends to write extensively related to business plans, vacationing, strategic planning, corporate finance and incorporating financial modeling into startup and expanding organizations.

Introduction

As a doctoral candidate, professional business consultant, and business plan writer, I am often asked by aspiring and seasoned entrepreneurs alike, "What is the first step for starting a restaurant business or expanding a current restaurant operation?".

When I first started out as a business consultant, I would explain to my client their place in the entrepreneurial process. I then support this analysis with proven academic and practicing business theory, along with recommending specific steps to take to start or expand their restaurant operations.

After going through this process time and time again with restaurant entrepreneurs, it dawned on me that the first step I ALWAYS recommend is writing a business plan.

Unfortunately, most restaurant entrepreneurs do not know how to write a professionally polished and structured restaurant business plan. Hell, most owners don't know how to write any type of business plan at all. From this issue, I decided to write this book focused on a ten-step process to writing a well-structured restaurant business plan.

The restaurant business plan writing steps include all aspects of the business plan writing process, beginning with developing the executive summary through constructing a professional and polished funding request.

In each step, I introduce you to a different restaurant business plan section. I then explain in layman's terms what the section means, offer a restaurant-specific business plan sample, and analyze the sample to help you understand the component. The objective of this detailed process is to ensure full understanding of each section and segment, with the goal of you being able to write a professional restaurant business plan for yourself, by yourself!

IF you still need help writing your restaurant business plan, at the end of the book, I ALSO supply you with a professionally written sample restaurant business plan AND a restaurant business plan template for you to use. On a final note, to put the cherry on top, **I have conducted and included preliminary restaurant market research for you** to use in your personalized plans!

In the end, I am supremely confident that this book, with the numerous tools and tips for restaurant business plan writing, will help you develop your coveted restaurant business plan in a timely fashion.

Step 1 – Restaurant Description

The restaurant description section of a business plan should thoroughly explain, in a nutshell, what the restaurant will do, how the firm will do it, where the restaurant will do it, and specific strategies that may, or may not, be used through the course of operations.

This sounds like a lot of information for just one section. And yes, it definitely is. This section, just about, is the only one devoted to thoroughly describing the inner workings of the restaurant.

Restaurant Summary:

The leadoff batter for this section is the restaurant summary. The purpose of a restaurant summary is to give the reader a broad understanding of the organization. In order to accomplish this feat, make sure to answer the questions: who, what, where, when, and how, in one or two paragraphs.

Business Plan Writing Tip:

When writing the restaurant summary, try to keep the section's content to a paragraph or two. Keep in mind; a business plan is a tool used for documenting the proposed business. However, due to internal and external forces in a restaurant's environment, (new products, competitors, etc.) providing too many details may lead to a plan that needs continuous updating.

A better practice, at least when starting up a restaurant, is to leave some wiggle room for changes. The best way to do this would be to keep the scope of writing broad. In other words, provide enough details, so the reader understands the business, but not so many aspects that the plan needs updating more than once every six months.

Sample:

Restaurant Summary

ABC Restaurant will be a limited liability corporation located at 123 Broadway St. in Orlando, FL. Our business owner(s) will be John Smith. Our casual dining breakfast restaurant will focus on popular breakfast menu items such as eggs with breakfast meats, pancakes, omelets, chicken and waffles, and more. As for a lunch menu, this includes popular sandwiches, burgers, and home-made soups. Our hours of operation will be from 6 AM To 2:30 PM, seven days a week.

Analysis:

The structure above succinctly shows the name of the restaurant, the type of legal structure for the business, menu items offered, location, and hours of operation. In other words, who, what, where, when, and how. Further, the information is kept to a paragraph. Short and sweet.

Competitive Advantages:

The competitive advantage for a restaurant is what the firm will do better than other competitors. As with most sections of the business plan, this concept may be interpreted in a multitude of ways. To illustrate, a competitive advantage may include differentiated men offerings, a prime location, or even an exceptional serving staff.

Business Plan Writing Tip:

Think about how the restaurant will be different from local competitors. Once you identify and state the differentiating factor, or factors, then explain why this is important for the business or to the customers.

Sample:

Competitive Advantages

ABC Restaurant will have specific competitive advantages once our firm starts operations. First, our restaurant will use local, farm-fresh produce and dairy products when possible. No other restaurant in the area has committed to this business model. Further, our firm will embrace the "fusion" concept in our menu items. For our fusion concept, we will offer both popular Mexican dishes, as well as, down-home Southern meals as a building block for our restaurant.

Analysis:

The first competitive advantage should always be the most important competitive advantage for the restaurant. When discussing this competitive advantage, make sure to explain, in detail, what the competitive advantage is and why it's essential. Also, be detailed but concise.

On a final note, always touch on one or two competitive advantages, but no more. The business plan should show some differentiation, but the differentiation should not seem to far outside of the norm. In other words, there are proven business models out there, use them and differentiate from them, but don't differentiate too much.

Product / Service Description:

In the product/service description section, make sure to thoroughly explain the product or service the restaurant will offer. To illustrate, a restaurant owner may list menu items and contents in each dish served. A menu item could be an "American Cheeseburger" and ingredients described as lettuce, tomato, mayonnaise, and American cheese. By doing this, the readers will fully understand the product and ingredients.

Business Plan Writing Tip:

Try not to exceed four or five services or products. Granted, a business plan should be thorough in this section. However, always keep in mind, the business plan should be balanced as well. Try not to have one section outweigh, in word-content, all of the other categories in the business plan. If the product or service offerings exceed five or six items, include the rest in an appendix.

Sample:

Product Description

Breakfast
Our breakfast menu items include omelets, pancakes, waffles, breakfast burritos, and Southern biscuits and gravy

Lunch:
For our lunch menu, we focus on sandwiches, soups, and burgers. Popular items include the "American Burger," topped with American cheese, lettuce, tomatoes, and pickles. Another popular lunch item will be our wide selection of soups.

Beverages:
Similar to other breakfast restaurants, we will offer traditional coffees, juices, and sodas.

For a full menu selection, please review Appendix A.

Analysis:

I chose to identify products and services as lunch, breakfast, and beverages. Under each subcategory, I briefly explain the possible menu offerings. The objective here is to help the reader understand menu offerings at various times throughout the day.

Pricing Strategy:

The pricing strategy section in a business plan should explain the business owner's thoughts and ideas in relations to how their prices compare to competitors. Popular pricing strategies may include low-cost leader, premium pricing, and a best value pricing approach.

The low-cost leader pricing approach is when product or services are priced slightly below local or regional restaurants. An excellent example of a low-cost leader would be McDonalds.

As for premium pricing, this would be when the business owner charges higher prices than area competitors, such as Ruth Chris Steakhouse. Often times, higher prices are justified due to differentiated services or higher quality menu ingredients.

In my most humble of opinions, my favorite pricing strategy, by far, is the best value approach. For this strategy, the management team will continually research the prices of comparable menu items offered by competitors in the area. From this research, the restaurant owner will then create a base price for each product or service using the averages of competitors in the area. Next, the organization will make price item adjustments based on the quality of the menu items or overall restaurant reputation as compared to yours. The end objective is to have all of your menu items priced competitively.

Business Plan Writing Tip:

When selecting a pricing strategy, make sure to use a financial model. By using a financial model, a restaurant owner can see the impact price changes may have on customer volume and net profits.

Pricing Strategy Example			
Item	Low Cost	Premium	Best Value
Number of Customers	100	50	75
Average Menu Price	22.00	35.00	30.00
Total Revenues	2,200.00	1,750.00	2,250.00
COGS	770.00	612.50	787.50
Gross Profit	1,430.00	1,137.50	1,462.50

In the example above, there are three different pricing strategies: low-cost, premium, and best value. Based on the financial model created, it looks like the best value approach will net the business owner the highest profits, even though the sales price is lower than premium pricing.

Sample:

Pricing Strategy

Our pricing structure will be focused on the best value strategy. For this strategy, our management team will continually research prices of comparable food and drink menu items offered by local restaurant competitors in the area. From this research, we will create base menu item prices using the averages of competitors in the area. Next, our organization will make menu item price adjustments based on the quality of ingredients, the ambiance of the competitors' eateries, and overall menu selection as compared to ours. The end objective is to have all of our menu item prices competitively priced using the best value strategic model.

Analysis:

This sample shows the business owner embracing the best value strategic pricing approach. Also, it emphasizes a specific strategy for implementing its pricing practice. The result is a well thought out strategy, which addresses the pricing segment of a business plan, as well as, allows for understanding the thought process behind the strategic pricing action.

Business Models:

One of my favorite sections to write in any business plan is the business model section. This is because a business model can be just about any action or process that makes a restaurant money. From this, business model sections vary significantly between restaurants.

Popular sections in my restaurant business model category may include discussions about food quality, hours of operation, number of workers, customer experience, or even the business owner's philosophy with treating employees or suppliers.

Business Plan Writing Tip:

When writing about business models, make sure to first identify the business model. Then discuss how the business model will operate. By doing this, restaurant owners can show how different aspects of their restaurant will impact their profits and or benefit customers.

Sample:

Business Models

Operations:
Our operational structure will seek to achieve a quick-service restaurant's speed of service while offering high-quality meals that would rival a casual dining experience. As a customer approaches our restaurant, they will be met with our menu posted on the door or chalkboard stand out front. This will allow visitors to decide upon their favorite dish before entering the restaurant.

At the counter, our customers will be able to point to and select food items for purchase. Once the selection process is complete, we cook the items and bring the food to the register for payment. In total, the process for each guest should be less than four minutes.

Hours of Operations:
Our hours of operations business model will be structured to ensure our restaurant customers' needs are met at a convenient time. From this, our organization will be open from 6 AM to 2:30 PM, seven days a week.

Analysis:

The example above is based on a general restaurant operation. Specifically, the perspective for the business model used was from the customer. By including the customer's perspective of operations, the owner can describe the customer's experience and show why the operational structure has been created to achieve the desired experience.

As for hours of operation, personally, I like to address this segment in the business model section as well. The strategy is utilized simply to keep operational business components in one section.

Location:

The location section of the business plan will definitely be structured differently, depending on the industry. Usually, in the location section, I will first note the restaurant's address. Once this is done, then a discussion about the inherent benefits of the location should be discussed. For example, make sure to discuss square footage, utilization of the square footage, and layout of the site. Once complete, next discuss the external benefits of the location. External benefits may include parking availability, proximity to your target market demographic, and distance from major thoroughfares.

Business Plan Writing Tip:

For most of my business plans, I prefer to include a map picture with the location address labeled. This helps to emphasize the external benefits for the location.

Sample:

Location

As previously stated, our location will be in the Orlando, Florida area. The proposed location size will be about 4,500 square feet. Approximately three-quarters of the area will be dedicated to the front of the house operations. The rest of the area will be devoted to the back of the house operations, office space, and storage.

As for competition, this area has few other Southern breakfast restaurants within a several miles radius. This will enable us to capture a significant portion of the casual dining breakfast restaurant market share in the area.

Analysis:

For my business plans, I like to label this subsection header in bold font. This helps the restaurant owner, or other readers, scan through the document and identify important pieces of information. Next, I always include the city and state, at a minimum, for the location. If a location has not been found, then the restaurant owner should outline the parameters needed for their operation. For this example, the restaurant owner needs approximately 4,500 ft.^{2} and the ability to divide the facility between the front of house operations and office space/kitchen space/storage.

The final component of the location I usually used to address, briefly, competition in the area. Keep in mind; if there is a thorough saturation of competitors in the area, I may skip over this component or explain why the location is best suited for the area.

Future Plans:

The future plan section should contain a discussion about the restaurant owner's thoughts and ideas for the future. The views may include expanding operations to new locations or adding new menu items. A popular discussion topic in this section is about opening a second or third location in the region. Regardless as to the firm's future plans, make sure to show a conceptual strategy for growth.

Business Plan Writing Tip:

My preference is to be rather ambiguous with future growth plans. For example, a restaurant owner may plan to open 4 or 5 new locations within the next five years. In this situation, explain in your plan that the restaurant will expand to several new locations within this timeframe. This shows that there are growth expectations. However, a specific number of new operations is held back.

Sample:

Future Plans

Within the next 24 months, our firm will open new locations in the Orlando / Central Florida area. The new sites and timeframe will be based on funding, leadership availability, and other factors. Further, our management team will introduce new menu items within the next 12 months. These menu items will be selected based on customer demand, how well the menu item will complement our current offering, and availability of fresh ingredients.

Analysis:

Notice that a specific timeframe is stated. This allows the business owner to set a deadline for when the expansion should be completed. Next, if the future plans include expansion, identify the general area in which the restaurant may grow. This helps to set specific parameters for geographic development. In this case, growing in the Central Florida area shows the business owner is seeking to exploit brand recognition in a specific centralized location.

Business Objectives and Time Line:

Every business will have specific objectives they wish to achieve. To accomplish the coveted objectives, restaurant owners need to list the objectives and have a specific deadlines for completion. What better way to categorize a list of objectives then to put them in a timeline?

By following this structure, not only will a restaurant owner be able to identify the objectives they need to accomplish, but the timeframe and order in which the objectives should be conquered.

Business Plan Writing Tip:

For this section, I like to break up the timeline into three to six-month timeframes. Further, when writing this section, I almost always start by developing the last time slot first. If my business objectives and timeline will cover up to two years, then I would start with the two-year point and work to the present. By following this strategy, the business owner can make sure each business objective aligns with the others.

Sample:

Business Objectives and Time Line

1 - 3 Months
- Obtain investor funding.
- Identify facility and negotiate a rental agreement.
- Engage in buildout activities.
- Open for business.

3 – 6 Months
- Start an advertising campaign.
- Evaluate marketing strategy and implement.
- Evaluate business models.

6 – 12 Months
- Optimize marketing strategies.
- Optimize business models.
- Examine external environment for market opportunities.

Analysis:

In the example above, I staggered the time frames between three months to six-month sections. The further out I went, timewise, the broader the timeframe. This is because almost all objectives past six months should be broad due to the continual fluctuation of market activities. In other words, stuff changes too much in business to have specific objectives past six months.

In contrast, for the first six months, try to be as specific as possible. As shown above, for the first three months, I have specific objectives listed in the order that they should be achieved. This helps the restaurant owner stay focused on a sequential set of tasks for the short-term.

Mission Statement:

The mission statement section of the business plan should succinctly describe what a restaurant will do to earn their revenues. Some restaurant owners like to focus on customer service as a center of their mission statement. Others prefer discussing the quality of ingredients used. Regardless, the mission statement needs to convey the restaurant owner's philosophy or mindset related to operations or customer service.

Business Plan Writing Tip:

The mission statement should be short enough so employees and customers will remember it. For my business's mission statement, I chose to focus on helping small business owners achieve their objectives.

Sample:

Mission Statement

"Our restaurant's mission is to provide the best Southern-style entrées in a friendly atmosphere and clean environment."

Analysis:

The sample started with identifying the restaurant's main offering, which is Southern-style meals. Next, the mission described the atmosphere they wish customers to enjoy, while at their establishment. This shows the restaurant will strive to continuously improve their products, while ensuring a predetermined ambiance for their guests.

Vision Statement:

The vision statement for a business plan focuses on how a restaurant will look in the distant future. Organizations may take a few different approaches to writing a vision statement. In the first approach, the statement may include number of employees at that point in time, geographic area serviced by the business, or brand recognition for the restaurant. In most instances, the timeframe is dated 3 to 5 years into the future.

A second method is to forgo a specific time frame and focus on an "impossible" vision. The impossible vision helps restaurant owners and employees continually strive to meet exceedingly high expectations.

Business Plan Writing Tip:

Selecting the vision statement format is pretty much a restaurant owners' preference. If a specific timeframe is used, then the vision may need to be updated periodically. For an 'impossible' vision, this type of statement is, more or less, static.

Sample:

Vision Statement

"Deliver world-class Southern breakfast delights on a global level."

Analysis:

For this vision statement, I chose the "impossible" vision route. What I mean by an impossible vision is that, objectively speaking, there is no way that a restaurant will accomplish the stated vision. However, from a motivational perspective, this overreaching vision will help keep the owner focused on expanding services to new areas.

Value Statement:

The value statement should highlight specific values the restaurant owner and employees embrace and practice on an unremitting basis. In this section, use bullet points to convey the values for the restaurant.

Business Plan Writing Tip:

This segment is pretty straightforward. Popular values may be honesty, high quality, technological innovation.

Sample:

Value Statement

- Honesty.
- Fair prices.
- High-quality dishes.
- Technical innovations

Analysis:

These values express the restaurant owner's commitment to fairness and honest business practices. As a rule, try to keep the value statement short and to the point.

Keys to Success:

Most business plans finish off the restaurant description section with a discussion about "Keys to Success." For this category, focus on the restaurant owner's perspective as to critical actions for success. Common keys to success include customer service, employee equality, and innovation. Again, in this section, use either bullet points or a graphical representation.

Business Plan Writing Tip:

Use a graphical representation in the section to succinctly show thoughts and ideas about the actions or concepts that the restaurant will embrace and is essential for its long-term success.

Sample:

Keys to Success

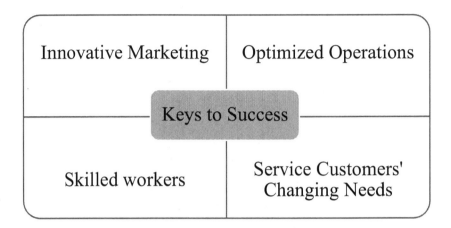

Analysis:

In the graphical representation, the star of the show is "Keys to Success." In each section, the key to success focused on a different aspect of the restaurant. Innovative marketing related to marketing actions, optimized operations to the restaurant's operational business models, etc. In other words, all keys to success are not focused on one area of the restaurant, but a range of different aspects for the facility.

Step 2 – Target Market

The target market section of a business plan should concentrate on a specific demographic or group of people, with similar traits or characteristics, that need or want the restaurant's services. At least, this is the "textbook" definition of the target market.

When I have my client described their target market, I like to set a scene for the client. The scenario goes something like this:

"You see a person walking towards you. There is no doubt in your mind that this person will absolutely, 100%, unequivocally stop in your restaurant. What does this person look like? Describe the person in as much detail as possible. "

Here are some helpful questions to answer.

- What does a person look like?
- Is the person male and female?
- Young or old?
- How are they dress? Blue-collar worker? Executive? Office worker?

Once a restaurant owner can identify their primary target market, they are now ready to complete the primary target market segment of the business plan.

On a final note, keep in mind, just because a restaurant entrepreneur has a narrow target market, it does not mean that this demographic will be their only customers. The organization very well may have a broad appeal to a multitude of demographics. However, every restaurant, has a limited amount of resources they can dedicate towards advertising. Because of the scarce resource, having a target market in mind who will best appeal to the restaurant's advertising dollars is definitely advisable.

Primary Target Market:

Most restaurants will have several demographics that appeal to their menu offerings and chosen theme. However, almost always, there is one demographic, or group of people, that will most definitely want the restaurant's core menu items. This demographic is the primary target market for the restaurant.

Business Plan Writing Tip:

Make sure to describe the primary target market in detail. Also, justify why this demographic was selected. Not only will this help you understand whom the firm is targeting for their menu items, but why this group was selected.

Sample:

Primary Target Market

Our primary target market will be young, blue color works. Specifically, females between the ages of 25 to 35. This demographic was selected because of their propensity to enjoy Southern breakfast cuisines while socializing with friends and family.

Analysis:

The primary target market identified in this example were female, blue-collar workers between the ages of 25 to 35 who enjoy Southern breakfast cuisines while socializing with friends and family. In this example, there is a specific age bracket, worker description, and appreciation noted for the organization's menu items.

Just by reading these couple of sentences, a person can visualize what the target market looks like. As noted above again, just because the target market is a narrow group of people does not mean the organization will not appeal to other demographics.

Identifying the primary target market will allow the restaurant owner to devise advertising campaigns that will appeal to this demographic. Further, a restaurant owner can decorate their establishment utilizing items that will appeal to this demographic.

Secondary Target Market:

The secondary target market should be written in a similar manner as the primary target market. Except, a separate demographic should be constructed. By following this process, the restaurant owner is showing that their facility will appeal to more than just one demographic. In other words, having a secondary target market indicates a broad appeal for the restaurant's offerings.

Sample:

Secondary Target Market

As for the secondary target market, this will be medical professionals working at the hospital across the street or in medical facilities surrounding the hospital. This demographic was selected due to their proximity to our restaurant.

Analysis:

In this example, a demographic was selected based on profession and geographic distance from our hypothetical restaurant. This shows that the restaurant will appeal to a wide area of people, as well as, niche, targeted groups.

Target Market Growth Potential:

Target market growth is another key component that should be addressed in the target market section of the business plan. Target market growth potential is how much growth a restaurant entrepreneur expects in their target market. Usually, this is measured in percentages or actual growth estimate numbers.

Business Plan Writing Tip:

When writing the target market growth potential segment of the business plan, I like to, personally, include a little bit of math. For example, if the blue-collar segment of the city is approximately 250,000 people, and the growth rate in the city has been 1.3% annually, we can then multiply the 250,000 by 1.013. This would give us a population target market 253,250 people in the next 12 months. This process may also be utilized in the same manner for subsequent years as well.

Sample:

Target Market Growth Potential

Based on research from website XYZ, the current blue color work force in ABC City is 250,000 people. The U.S. Census Bureau has noted that the city's population increased by 1.3% annually over the last five years. Based on this factor, our restaurant owner expects a similar growth rate for the next five years. From this, the target market formulation will be 253,250 within the next 12 months. In two years, our target market population will expand to 256,543 people.

Analysis:

The important take away in the segment is that the restaurant owner's assumptions, which are the population growth rate and the number of blue-collar workers, are sourced. By showing where your information comes from, the entrepreneur is adding credibility to the assumptions. The math, obviously, stands for itself.

Step 3– Market Analysis

The market analysis section of the business plan should address and examine the external aspects of the restaurant. Common external aspects of business would include the business's industry, competitor review, and possibly a discussion about the economy and its potential effects on the industry as a whole.

Industry Overview:

Identify the main industry the business completes, in this case the restaurant industry. Once the industry is identified, then try and determine if there are sub-industries, with enough data, that aligns with your dining concept. For example, in the restaurant industry, subcategories include food trucks, casual dining, and quick service establishments. With this done, now research and take notes about the statistics and trends, such as total industry sales, growth rates for the industry, and popular tends currently being exploited.

Business Plan Writing Tip:

Thoroughly describe the characteristics and trends in the industry. For example, in the restaurant industry, common characteristics would be growth rates, the price range of the menu items, and new restaurant themes like gastropubs or food halls.

Sample:

Juice and smoothie bars sell fruit drinks, protein shakes, vegetable drinks, and other healthy food and drink items. The foodservice industry, as a whole, should exceed $5 billion next year. The juice and smoothie bars industry, which is a sub section of the foodservice industry, will reach over $3 billion in sales for 2019. For the next several years, industry experts project annual revenue growth of approximately 1.8%.

Analysis:

This example started with explaining the specific characteristics commonly displayed by competitors in the industry. Next, a brief revenues and growth discussion of the overall industry was offered. This then led to addressing the potential revenues for the subsection industry, as well as, the potential growth rate for the future.

Industry Statistics:

Industry statistics may focus on a wide array of topics. A great way to start the restaurant statistic segment is just do an internet search about the industry and its statistics. Once this is complete, start reading articles and taking notes about the industry and specific statistics.

In going through this process, not only will the business owner deepen their knowledge about the industry, but they will also be able to show, through writing, in-depth research was done on the topic.

Business Plan Writing Tip:

When writing this section, I prefer to utilize bullet points to show statistics about the restaurant industry.

Sample:

Statistics

- Studies have shown that close to 30% of all US adults do not meet or exceed their daily servings of vegetables and fruit.

- On a global basis, juice bar sales have exceeded $9 billion.

- Premium juice sales have grown by approximately 11% since 2000.

- 83% of consumers have stated that a fruit-based smoothie is preferable as compared to a dairy base.

Analysis:

This example shows various statistics in relations to the juice and smoothie bar industry. As you can see, the structure utilized is a bullet point format. To take it a step further, make sure to utilize footnotes for citations. This will add credibility to your statistics section.

Threats, Trends, and Opportunities:

The trends, threats, and opportunity section are an excellent opportunity for the restaurant owner to show how "in tune" they are with customer trends, and industry opportunities. When I write this section for clients, I usually like to equalize the information with an even number of threats, trends, and opportunities. This shows a well-balanced and researched section.

Business Plan Writing Tip:

Even though "opportunities" is listed last in the title, I often start this section by discussing opportunities in the marketplace first. Opportunities in an industry may be found in a multitude of ways. Some restaurant owners survey potential customers to find out their needs. Other business owners will network with regional or national competitors to identify industry opportunities. Regardless of how opportunities are identified, make sure to thoroughly explain your findings.

As for structure, I prefer to use paragraph form for addressing the threats, trends, and opportunities.

Sample:

Trends, Threats, and Opportunities

An important threat to an industry would be related to the overall economy. Currently, job growth and employment are at all-time-highs. From this, people have enough discretionary funds to afford dining out. Unfortunately, in the event of an economic recession, as discretionary funds for people decrease, profits for the restaurant industry may show a correlated effect.

As for an opportunity, casual dinners are increasing selecting "mom and pop" restaurants over chain restaurants due to better service and appealing menu selections. This allows for startup restaurants to enter the market place and gain a loyal following. Finally, trends in the restaurant industry may be found in technological innovations. Technological innovations may help restaurant owners offer better-quality foods or enhanced service for premium prices.

Analysis:

Each topic, trend, threat, and opportunity were given equal attention. Also, thorough explanations were provided to support each finding.

Keys to Success:

The industry "keys to success" section will different as compared to the "keys to success" discussion found in the restaurant description category. As noted in the restaurant's description, the keys to success were written based on the business owner's perspective of the restaurant. In contrast, the industry section keys to success utilize research, and the perspective employed should be from the restaurant industry as a whole. In other words, what are most of your competitors doing, and doing well, in order to be successful in the industry?

Business Plan Writing Tip:

For this section, make sure to do research and take notes. When I write a keys to success section for the industry, I often review articles related to industry leaders. As I go through the articles, I will jot down notes related to actions they have taken to be successful. After I have gone through several articles, I then compare the notes with the objective of finding commonalities. To illustrate, for restaurants, an important key to success is a themed presentation.   Just look at Olive Garden, Outback, or Mello Mushroom.

Sample:

Keys to Success

To be successful in the restaurant industry, competitors need to focus on hiring skilled employees. In other words, small businesses must employ and retain qualified and well-trained workers. Qualifications may not necessarily be in traditional schooling.   However, experience with kitchen prep, serving, and hosting is necessitated to ensure that a guest has a memorable visit to a restaurant.

Analysis:

In this example, the keys to success were focused on a small business owner competing in the restaurant industry. An important identification, based on industry research, was the need for skilled workers. With this as a foundation, a brief reflection as to why this fact was focused on was needed.

SWOT Analysis:

The SWOT analysis is a popular strategic tool used by restaurant owners to quickly and broadly identify different aspects of the restaurant's internal and external environments. Unfortunately, most restaurant owners utilize the SWOT analysis incorrectly.

The SWOT analysis is broken up into four segments, which are strengths, weaknesses, opportunities, and threats. This is common knowledge for most small restaurant owners. However, what most small businesses owners do not know is that the strengths and weaknesses are one category and opportunities and threats are a second.

In the strength and weaknesses segment, the restaurant owner should focus on the internal aspects of their business.   What are the restaurant's strengths and weaknesses? For the opportunities and threats section, this is where the owner examines their external environment, seeking out opportunities and potential threats to the organization.

Business Plan Writing Tip:

Make sure to utilize a visually appealing format, bullet points, and always, always have at least twice as many strengths and opportunities as compared to weaknesses and threats.

Sample:

Strengths
Management experience.
Documented plans
Themed restaurant
   concept
Training program

Weakness
Startup restaurant.
Untested business
   location.

Opportunities
Community involvement
Appeal to a wide variety
   of clientele.
Location
Brand building

Threats
Local competitors
Susceptible to
   economic downturn.

Analysis:

Most important fact to identify is the strength and weakness section focused on the internal aspects of the restaurant. Whereas opportunities and threats segments concentrated on the external environment.

Competitive Analysis:

The competitive analysis section is where the restaurant owner has an opportunity to examine and discuss local or regional competitors. This section may be as short as listing competing restaurants, their distance from the target facility, and a paragraph summarizing the competitors' strengths and weaknesses. Or, this segment may be a full-blown competitive analysis analyzing important segments of each competitors' restaurant operation. For most restaurant owners, the former approach is often best.

Business Plan Writing Tip:

The competitive analysis section, in my most humble of opinions, should be short and sweet. The preferred structure that I use is to identify the competitor's name, address, hours of operation, and a website link. With this completed, I then analyze the competition from a customer's perspective. To do this, just review the competitor's website and Google/Facebook reviews about the restaurant. In following this structure, the restaurant owner is able to gain important perspectives as to how the competition operates and, potentially, their glaring strengths and weaknesses.

Sample:

Dine Here Restaurant is a "mom and pop" restaurant in the Washington DC. area. The restaurant was founded in 1984 and prides themselves on their 24hr availability. As for services, the diner offers a limited menu, focused on breakfast, lunch, and dinner. Based on a Google search, customers have had mixed reviews. Most reviews seemed satisfied with the diner's food quality and service. However, some past customers complained that the cleanliness of the facility was lacking.

Analysis:

The short paragraph above succinctly noted the name of the competitor, a brief background of the competitor, if available, and a short discussion related to how customers perceive the organization.

Step 4 – Organization and Management

The organization and management section should be used to discuss the business structure of the restaurant, management team, and job responsibilities.

Management Summary:

In the management summary section, most restaurant owners will include a brief bio about the founder and the management team. When writing the bio, make sure to highlight skills and experiences that are associated the restaurant or perspective industry.

Business Plan Writing Tip:

Some restaurant owners like to believe that their business is all about them. And for a lot of small restaurants, it is. However, if you examine the egocentric concept from an investor perspective, if something happens to the restaurant owner, then the investor may lose their investment because the business would not be able to continue.

Because of this important issue, try to keep the bio section at a paragraph or less each for the founder and executive team. This is enough information to demonstrate experience and competence. But, not so much information that the restaurant owner and management team become the star of the show as compared to the business.

Sample:

Owner Bio

John Smith, Sr., MBA., is the founder and CEO of ABC Restaurant. He has started and managed numerous successful small restaurants over the last ten years. Restaurants started, and managed, includes a breakfast cafe, food truck, and 24 hour diner. For each business, he was responsible for all aspects of the organizations, from marketing to strategic planning.

Analysis:

The brief bio first identifies the person discussed and their job title. Following this introduction, a brief discussion about experiences was made. This showed the owner has qualifications for the new restaurant and has supporting experiences as well.

Job Responsibilities:

Job responsibilities section is mainly included to help the restaurant owner demonstrate an in-depth understanding about the restaurant structure and document potential positions needed. Further, by discussing and identifying job responsibilities, the restaurant owner can alleviate future disagreements between the executive team members. This is done by explicitly stating job responsibilities for the business owner, executive team members, and hourly staff.

Business Plan Writing Tip:

For larger restaurants, not all positions and job descriptions should be included. For example, a restaurant job responsibility section might list the executive team positions, chefs, kitchen help, servers, and host position. This indicates that the business owner has at least a basic knowledge of the different positions needed for the restaurant.

Sample:

Job Positions and Responsibilities

CEO:
- Create and execute marketing strategies for restaurant growth.
- Align restaurant strategies with the vision statement.
- Negotiating contracts with vendors.

- Ensure legal compliance for the restaurant.
- Continually examine the firm's external environment for new market opportunities.

General Manager:
- Control inventory to ensure optimal levels are attained.
- Manage day-to-day operations of the restaurant.
- Servers and cooks during high volume times.
- Interview and hire new employees.
- Assist in the onboarding process for new employees.

Analysis:

For each job position, make sure not to list more than four or five functions performed. This structure helps to limit too much discussion about any one job position. Further, by staying broad with the descriptions, the restaurant owner is able to not reveal too much about their operational structure and strategies.

Step 5 – Organizational Chart

The organizational chart section is pretty much a visual representation of the job responsibility section. The objectives here are to show each business position within the restaurant, visually. Also, this structure helps to convey the chain of command for the proposed restaurant.

Organizational Chart:

The organizational chart should visually show each position within the restaurant as well as whom that position reports.

Business Plan Writing Tip:

The honest truth is that most people will not read the job responsibility section. However, when individuals, such as employees, come across graphs or charts, they tend to spend a little bit of time assessing the information. From this, a well-prepared organizational chart will visually educate folks about the different positions in the restaurant and the chain of command expected.

Sample:

Organizational Chart

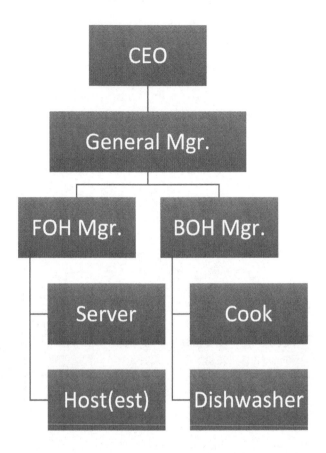

Analysis:

The chart above showed the CEO as the leader in the organization. The chain of command then moved to the store manager and assistant manager. The thorough example illustrated that both the front and back of house workers will report to the assistant manager.

Step 6 – Marketing

In the marketing section, the restaurant owner has the opportunity to describe their thoughts and ideas about how the firm is going to connect with their target market. Popular forms of marketing may include social media, website, and traditional advertising opportunities. In most instances, restaurant owners are going to exploit each one of the marketing channels in order to reach their target market on multiple platforms.

Marketing Objectives and Keys to Success:

In the marketing objectives and keys to success section, I like to use a visual representation showing the company's marketing objectives, as well as, identifying specific actions that the restaurant owner needs to take in order to be successful.

Business Plan Writing Tip:

When writing this section, I always utilize a visual representation. This helps me convey, succinctly, my thoughts and ideas related to marketing and the objectives that need to be attained through the actions.

Sample:

Objectives	Keys to Success
Market penetration.	Selecting appropriate marketing channels.
Brand awareness.	Continually keep customers engaged with our marketing material.
Meet customers' changing needs.	
Create marketing synergy	Periodically evaluate marketing actions for optimization.

Analysis:

In the marketing objectives section, popular objectives for restaurants may include market penetration, brand building, or educating customers in relations to the menu items offered. As for keys to success, my preference is to focus on general actions that a restaurant needs to take in order to achieve their objectives. For example, if a restaurant selects the appropriate marketing channels, then the firm will achieve brand awareness.

Traditional Marketing:

Traditional marketing channels may include mailers, signage, and networking. Depending on your restaurant location and theme, even your personality type, one or all of the traditional market opportunities may be exploited.

Business Plan Writing Tip:

Make sure to list and discuss all your thoughts and ideas as to the different types of traditional marketing you may implement at some point in time. Just because you may not do mailers immediately, still address this in the business plan and, in general terms, discuss your thoughts and ideas in relations to the topic.

Sample:

Traditional Marketing

Our first traditional marketing channel will include a professionally designed sign for the front of the restaurant. This sign will include our restaurant name, logo, and slogan. Further, prominent colors will include black, gold, and white. The objective of the signage is to let potential customers know our restaurant's theme and possible menu items offered.

Analysis:

In most parts of the business plan, I have a strong preference for being vague and using general descriptions. This is because entrepreneurs are, and should be, paranoid about competitors finding out their strategies. However, for advertising, once a marketing campaign hits, competitors are definitely going to know the strategic thoughts and ideas behind the marketing action. From this simple fact, in the business plan, go ahead and be detailed with your traditional in other types of marketing thoughts and ideas.

Internet Marketing:

Internet marketing is any type of marketing using the internet. Common Internet marketing actions may include developing a website, blogs, Google, or Bing paid advertising, and yelp postings.

Business Plan Writing Tip:

When writing about your Internet advertising, trying to touch on all aspects of Internet advertising that you wish to implement. For example, if you are going to have a website, make sure to talk about it, if you are going to register with Yelp, or other business directories, then make sure to include this information in the business plan as well. By using this strategy, a business owner can show a broad understanding of potential internet marketing channels.

Sample:

Internet Marketing

The importance of a professionally designed website cannot be understated. To exploit this opportunity, XYZ Restaurant will create and maintain a website and Yelp listing. The objective for the strategy is to effectively communicate our restaurant's theme and highlight our menu items.

Analysis:

I identified two specific Internet advertising channels that will be exploited. The channels are a business directory, which is Yelp, and the website. Further, the objectives of Internet advertising were discussed.

Social Media Marketing:

One of the hottest and most popular forms of advertising currently is social media. Social media advertising channels may include Facebook, Instagram, and Twitter. Because of social media's popularity, new channels are continually entering the market and trending with potential customers. From this, restaurant owners should not only explore and discuss using current social media channels but also review strategies to exploit new social media opportunities as well.

Business Plan Writing Tip:

A restaurant owner may choose to discuss each social media advertising channel separately or go broad and outline strategic actions that may be employed in all social media channels.

Sample:

Social Media Marketing

ABC Restaurant's social media advertising will include Instagram, Twitter, and Facebook. Using a three-channel approach to social media will ensure our message reaches a broad audience, which will include our target market. In addition, several potential customers will receive an advertising message on multiple social media outlets. This should exceed the needed repetition of our message to a broad audience as well as our target market. The marketing message will focus on our restaurant menu items offered, and possible weekly specials.

Analysis:

In the example above, our fictitious restaurant owner first introduced the different social media outlets the firm will employ. Once this was complete, the restaurant owner explained, briefly, the strategy behind the social media actions. The final sentence touched on possible advertising content.

Step 7 – Financials

The financial statement section is probably the most difficult section for restaurant owners to write. There are numerous reasons for this fact. First, financial statements are mostly made in Excel. Most restaurant owners do not even have Excel on their computer, let alone, know how to use the various functions needed to create financial statements.

Another common challenge with creating financial statements in Excel is the need to intertwine different pages. For example, when I create my financial statements, I often use one page, or tab, as an information page. The rest of the pages, located on different tabs, are tied into the information page using links and formulas. By doing this, if I change a financial figure on the information page, all of the financial statements are updated.

Financial Assumptions:

Regardless of how much time you spend on the financial statements, you will not be able to escape the simple fact that your financial statements will be wrong. I like to tell my clients that I have been writing business plans for more than ten years and there is no way that I will know how many business plan appointments I will land tomorrow, let alone, what my revenues will be in a year.

Because of this unknown, I create my financial statements based on expected revenues starting at day one. From this point, I will grow the revenues based on expected growth rates, which will be discussed in a bit.

In order to explain to the reader where the financial statement results came from, an assumption page is needed. The assumption page just tells the reader what your assumptions are for the financial statements. Common assumptions include daily sales and costs, monthly fixed costs, growth rates, tax rate, number of employees, and the cost of goods sold.

Business Plan Writing Tip:

When writing your financial assumptions page, make sure to explain any assumptions used in the financial statement calculations, starting with the top line of your income statement and ending with the bottom line of your balance sheet. For example, when I list my assumptions for clients, I usually start with the expected monthly growth estimates. From this point, I outline expected cost of goods, the advertising budget, and so on. The objective of this outline is to establish credibility for your financial statements.

Sample:

Assumptions

Our financial projections have several assumptions based on research and management's expectation of potential sales and costs.

- All financial projections are based on management and or owner(s) professional expectations of sales and expenses for the foreseeable future.

- In the first 12 months, sales should increase by approximately 5% each month. In months 13 to 24, sales growth should slow to approximately .3% per month. For years three through five, sales are expected to grow by 4.5%.

- The cost of goods or variable costs are expected to be approximately 30.21% of total sales.

- The initial advertising budget will be $7,5000. Advertising is projected to increase by approximately 1% per year. This is to ensure maximum utilization of the firm's property and equipment.

- Cost projections were calculated using a common size model. This practice is typical for financial modeling.

- The tax rate was assumed to be 20%. Fluctuation in the tax rate will have a direct impact on net profits.

- Initial funding needed is 1,500,000. An increase/decrease in amount will impact the net present value and internal rate of return.

- Starting cash balance needed is $125,000 for working capital.

- Cash account was used to balance assets with liabilities and equity.

Analysis:

In the example above, one of the first actions done was to educate and disclose the growth rate expected on a monthly basis for the first year. Further, the example went into more details as to the reduction in the growth rate for the second year. By explaining the different growth rates, the business owner is able to show how financial sales were built.

The rest of the information just talked about various aspects of the financial statements, such as the cost of goods sold, starting budget for advertising, tax rate, initial funding, and cash that will be in the bank once the doors open for working capital. This structure lays the foundation for the business owner to justify their financial statements.

Financial Summary:

The financial summary should explain the highlights related to financial projections. These highlights include revenues and profits for the first year, expected profits for years two and five, and, when seeking funds from an investor, possibly the expected return on equity.

Business Plan Writing Tip:

When writing the financial summary section, first start off by explaining that the financial section of your business plan is based on research and observations. This disclaimer helps to set the stage for the reader's understanding that the projections are just the restaurant owner's best guesses. Next, follow-up the statement with your findings from your financial analysis. These findings should include revenues for the first year, net profits, and the profit margin expected.

Sample:

Financial Summary

The financial projections are based on market research and empirical examination of the local restaurant industry. For the next year, we project revenues of approximately $456,793. The estimated expense costs will be $217,330. After taxes, we estimate a net profit of $239,463. This leads to a profit margin of approximately 52.4%. As our brand continues to grow, second-year progression is anticipated to yield a net income of approximately $311,363. Within five years, net income should exceed $348,722.

Analysis:

In this example, the organization expected first-year revenues to exceed $450,000. Further, the cost involved in attaining these revenues were also shown. This helps the reader understand the potential revenue generation opportunities for the restaurant and the needed cost to achieve the dollar amount noted. Other important aspects of the summary would include the net profits for years two and five.

Startup/Expansion Costs:

The startup cost section of the business plan should include the costs needed to start the restaurant. If the business is already established, then this segment should outline expansion costs. If funding is being sought and the money will be used for purposes other than startup or expansion, then make sure to use this section to reflect how the money will be spent. An example of this would be if a restaurant needs funds to spend on an advertising campaign, then use the section to break down the costs for the campaign implementation.

Sample:

Startup Costs	
Category	**Estimate**
Equity Investment	1,000,000.00
Loan	500,000.00
Initial Build Out	900,000
Working Capital	125,000.00
Section: Equipment	
Restaurant Equipment (General)	75,000.00
FOH Equipment	35,000.00
BOH Equipment	40,000.00
Sub Total	150,000.00
Section: Operations	
Inventory	95,000.00
Supplies	150,000.00
Décor	28,000.00
Sub Total	273,000.00
Section: Office Equipment	
Office Equipment	25,000.00
Furniture	12,000.00
Sub Total	37,000.00
Section: Other	

Misc. Licenses	15,000.00
Sub Total	15,000.00
Total	**1,500,000.00**

Analysis:

When I set up my startup costs section, the first segment is always related to how much money the restaurant owner has invested, funds needed from an investor, desired loan amount, if a loan is needed, initial buildout, and working capital, which are funds used for operations when the business opens.

It may be considered a little unorthodox to include funding with startup costs. However, by following this structure, the restaurant owner succinctly showed funding needed and how the funds will be spent.

The rest of the sections focused on specific costs needed to start the restaurant. The specific categories used were equipment, operations, office equipment, and other. In these categories, I strongly suggest that the cost estimates be inflated a bit. Say by 10 to 20 percent. Further, try to stay "general" with startup costs. This strategy is recommended simply because there is no way to know what your actual startup costs will be until your startup process has commenced.

Daily Revenues:

For my daily revenues, I always start with estimating revenues and the cost of goods for the first day of business. Revenues are the sales price multiplied by the actual number of menu items sold. For the cost of goods, this is considered the dollar amount that the restaurant spent to make the product or service. For simplicity sake, I always utilize a percent for the cost of goods. This helps for staying true to using averages in the financial statements.

Business Plan Writing Tip:

When designing the average daily sales segment, always use averages for everything. By embracing the concept of using averages in the financial statements, the restaurant owner is acknowledging that the estimates provided in the financial statements are a best guess approximate as to what the business owner hopes to sell in the future.

Sample:

Average Daily Sales							
Revenue Generators							
Daily Sales	% Sales	Num.	Price	Cost	Profit	Total Rev.	Total Cost
Breakfast Sand.	20%	90	9.50	1.90	7.60	855	171
Platters	20%	90	13.50	2.70	10.80	1,215	243
Other	20%	120	7.50	1.50	6.00	900	180
Lunch and Dinner Entrees	30%	165	14.50	4.35	10.15	2,392	717.75
Side items	50%	60	7.50	3.75	3.75	450	225
Other	50%	90	6.50	3.25	3.25	585	292.5
					Total	6,398	1,829

Analysis:

In the first column, this is where I put the general categories for menu items the restaurant will sell. The first section is focused on breakfast menu items, such as breakfast sandwiches, platters, and other. Of course, there are further differentiating factors between the breakfast sandwiches and platters. However, for the sake of estimates, I use an average price for all breakfast sandwiches, platters, and so forth. In section 2, I broke up the category into lunch and dinner menu items sold, which would be the entrées and sides.

The second important item in the chart above would be "% Sales." The percent sales are used to determine the cost of goods sold. The cost of goods sold is how much the restaurant owner spends in order to make the menu items. To illustrate, the cost of goods sold may be the amount of money the restaurant spent on lettuce, tomatoes, and cucumbers.

Labor:

Every business that has ever been started, that will ever be started, needs some type of labor involved. Even if the labor is only the restaurant owner, make sure to include the labor section and the expected dollar amount to be paid on a monthly basis.

Sample:

Labor				
Employee	**Number**	**Rate**	**Monthly Hours**	**Total Pay**
Salary		n/a	n/a	4,500
Manager	1	25.00	172	4,300
Employees	18	18.00	172	55,728
			Total	60,028

Analysis:

When I create my labor template, the first line, salary, is the amount of money the restaurant owner wishes to be compensated for their time and energy. Some owners may argue that they will not take a salary in the first year. However, lenders and investors, almost to the person, will want to see the owner take some kind of salary when the restaurant starts. Because of this, the salary is always the first line in all of my labor financial models.

Following this line item would be managers and employees. As you can see in the example above, the structure will allow you to enter the number of managers in the average pay rate as well as the number of employees and their average pay rate. Again, we are embracing and exploiting the concept of averages.

Monthly Fixed Costs:

The monthly fixed cost segment should include any and all costs that the restaurant will spend, continuously, on a monthly basis. Popular fixed costs may include rent, utilities, insurance, and advertising.

Sample:

Monthly Fixed Costs	
Monthly Costs	**Monthly Total**
Rent	15,000
Utilities	1,580
Office Expenses	780
Insurance	400
Accounting/legal	250
Advertising	7500
Other	650
Monthly Total	26,160

Analysis:

Fixed costs are definitely a misnomer. Just because we call them "fixed costs" does not mean the costs will not change on a monthly basis. The fixed costs title is more focused on the actual items being paid as compared to the same dollar amount paid each month.

When constructing the fixed costs segment, there are a couple of different theories that may be applied to the construction of the segment. First, some restaurant owners prefer to leave fixed cost as the same dollar amount throughout the year and then add a growth estimate for the next year.

Other owners prefer to utilize a percent of sales approach. In this approach, costs that change on a monthly basis, such as utilities, office expenses, and "other," would be based on a percent of sales technique. In this technique, each variable line item would be divided by sales. For subsequent months fixed costs, the line items would be calculated by multiplying the percent found in the first month for the line item by sales in the following months. This technique is known as common sizing.

Growth Rates:

Growth rates are the percentages used to increase a line item due to growth or inflation. Not surprisingly, different sections of the financial estimates will grow at different paces. From this, the need for a section related to growth rates is needed.

Sample:

Growth Rates	
Growth Rate Sales 2 & 3	3.50%
Growth Rate Sales 4 & 5	1.50%
Growth Rate Cost of Goods	1.50%
Growth Rate Salary	1.50%
Growth Rate Labor	3.00%
Growth Advertising	1.00%
Growth Office	1.00%
Growth Utility	1.00%
Growth Legal	1.00%

Growth Insurance	1.00%
Growth Other	1.00%

Analysis:

My preference for the growth rates is to show different growth rates for each category. Labor is bound to grow at a different pace than say business insurance. This structure allows for the needed adjustments.

Misc. Information:

The miscellaneous information section is pretty much used as a catchall for adjusting various line items in the financial statements. This segment may include the tax rate, cost of capital for the restaurant, franchise royalty payments, etc.

Sample:

Misc. Information	
Tax Rate	20%
Cost of Capital	10%

Analysis:

In this section, I usually only include the tax rate and cost of capital. For most instances, the cost of capital is not really needed. However, the tax rate is essential for determining estimated taxes that the restaurant will pay on a monthly and annual basis.

Loan Payment Calculation:

When obtaining a loan, banks often prefer to calculate the loan information using their proprietary software. However, the business owner should still use the Excel function for calculating payments and include the information in their financial statements. An important concept to keep in mind for the income statement is to make sure they subtract interest paid instead of the full monthly payment for the loan. Not only is this standard procedure for accounting, but it also helps to show increased revenues.

Sample:

Loan Information	
Loan Amount	(500,000.00)
Interest Rate	7%
Term	25
Payment	$3,533.90

Analysis:

In this example above, a loan is expected to be taken out for $500,000. The interest rate is expected to be 7% with a term of 25 years. As a result, the restaurant owner will be expected to pay $3,533.90 on a monthly basis. As noted above, for the profit and loss statement as well as the income statement, the monthly interest payment is the portion used. To find the interest portion, the amortization schedule is needed.

Profit and Loss for 12 Months:

The profit and loss statement show the revenues, costs, taxes, and profits for your restaurant. My preference is to break up the 12-month profit and loss statement into monthly segments and then total each month quarterly. By doing this, the restaurant owner is able to see the monthly growth projections, as well as, the costs aligned with the projected revenues.

Business Plan Writing Tip:

When creating your 12-month profit and loss statement, make sure to always use Excel or some other spreadsheet. This will allow you to do calculations easily and duplicate your work month over month.

When creating your profit and loss statement, make sure to always start with your revenues and then align the cost of goods and other fixed cost with your monthly sales. By following this process, the restaurant owner is able to see how much money the restaurant can make and what costs are involved with the process.

Sample:

Pro Forma Income Statement Year 1 Quarter 1				
	Month 1	**Month 2**	**Month 3**	**Quarter 1**
Revenues	192,941	198,729	204,691	596,361
COGS	57,145	58,859	60,625	176,629
Gross Profit	135,796	139,870	144,066	419,732
Expenses				
Salary	4,500	4,500	4,500	13,500
Labor	60,028	60,028	60,028	180,084
Advertising	7,500	7,500	7,500	22,500
Office Expen.	780	803	828	2,411
Rent	15,000	15,000	15,000	45,000
Utilities	1,580	1,627	1,676	4,884
Legal / Account	250	250	250	750
Insurance	400	400	400	1,200
Depreciation	11,667	11,667	11,667	35,000
Other	650	650	650	1,950
Total				

Expenses	102,355	102,425	102,498	307,279
EBIT	33,441	37,445	41,568	112,454
Interest Expense	2,917	2,913	2,909	8,739
EBT	30,525	34,532	38,658	103,715
Taxes	6,105	6,906	7,732	20,743
Net Income	24,420	27,625	30,927	82,972

Pro Forma Income Statement - Common Size				
Income Statement	Month 1	Month 2	Month 3	Quarter 1
Sales Growth	3.00%	3.00%	3.00%	6.09%
Revenues	100.00%	100.00%	100.00%	100.00%
Costs of goods Sold	29.62%	29.62%	29.62%	29.62%
Gross Profit	70.38%	70.38%	70.38%	70.38%
Expenses				
Salary	2.33%	2.26%	2.20%	2.20%
Labor	31.11%	31.11%	31.11%	31.11%
Advertising	3.89%	3.89%	3.89%	3.89%
Office Expenses	0.40%	0.40%	0.40%	0.40%
Rent	7.77%	7.77%	7.77%	7.77%
Utilities	0.82%	0.82%	0.82%	0.82%
Legal / Accounting	0.13%	0.13%	0.13%	0.13%
Insurance	0.21%	0.21%	0.21%	0.21%
Depreciation	6.05%	6.05%	6.05%	6.05%
Other	0.34%	0.34%	0.34%	0.34%

Total Expenses	53.05%	51.54%	50.07%	51.53%
EBIT	17.33%	18.84%	20.31%	18.86%
Interest Expense	1.51%	1.47%	1.42%	1.47%
Earnings before taxes	15.82%	17.38%	18.89%	17.39%
Taxes	3.16%	3.48%	3.78%	3.48%
Net Income	12.66%	13.90%	15.11%	13.91%

Analysis:

In this example, first start with the revenues that are projected for the month. In order to give first-month revenues, I always go back to my expected daily sales. Using the daily sales, I will then multiply the daily sales by 30 and the cost of goods by 30. This will give me my first-month sales and the cost of goods.

Next, identify the fixed costs aligned with the monthly sales and deduct them from the gross profits, which is just revenue subtracted by the cost of goods sold. Once this is complete, just subtract any interest expenses and taxes. This leaves the restaurant's net income.

To determine the second-month profit and loss, first start by multiplying the revenues by an expected monthly growth rate. Next, for costs that increase on a monthly basis, based on sales, use the common size financial document. For example, in the example above, the office expense was .4% of sales. From this, we would multiply .4% by the new revenues for the next 12-months to determine the expected office supplies costs. This practice would be used for labor, office expenses, and utilities as well. Keep in mind, for some costs, such as rent, advertising, insurance, and salary; these costs will remain the same, usually, for the first 12-months.

Income Statement:

The income statement is simply the total of your 12 months profit and loss statements. In other words, the income statement shows the total revenues and costs for the first 12-months. Once this is complete, most income statements will then project revenues, costs, and profits for the next four years, giving the restaurant owner a five-year income statement projection to review.

Business Plan Writing Tip:

When creating your income statement, my preference is to first construct a table showing quarterly profit and losses, as shown below. Next, total the quarterly profits and losses into an annual column. With this complete, create a table using the annual revenues, costs and include columns for years two through five. The next step is to utilize our growth projections, as noted earlier, and multiply each line item by the associated growth projection. This will result in a five-year income statement, as shown below.

Sample:

Pro Forma Income Statement Annual Summary					
	Quarter 1	Quarter 2	Quarter 3	Quarter 4	Annual
Revenues	596,361	651,660	712,087	778,116	2,738,224
COGS	176,629	193,007	210,904	230,461	811,001
Gross Profit	419,732	458,653	501,182	547,655	1,927,223
	-	-	-	-	-
Expenses					
Salary	13,500	13,500	13,500	13,500	54,000
Labor	180,084	180,084	180,084	180,084	720,336
Advertising	22,500	22,500	22,500	22,500	90,000
Office Expen.	2,411	2,610	2,852	3,116	10,988
Rent					180,000

	45,000	45,000	45,000	45,000	
Utilities	4,884	5,286	5,776	6,312	22,258
Legal / Account	750	750	750	750	3,000
Insurance	1,200	1,200	1,200	1,200	4,800
Deprec.	35,000	35,000	35,000	35,000	140,000
Other	1,950	1,950	1,950	1,950	7,800
Total Expenses	307,279	307,880	308,612	309,412	1,233,182
	-	-	-	-	-
EBIT	112,454	150,773	192,570	238,243	694,041
Interest Expense	8,739	8,706	8,673	8,639	34,758
EBT	103,715	142,067	183,897	229,604	659,283
Taxes	20,743	28,413	36,779	45,921	131,857
Net Income	82,972	113,653	147,118	183,684	527,426

Pro Forma Income Statement - Base					
	Year 1	Year 2	Year 3	Year 4	Year 5
Revenues	2,738,224	3,266,320	3,380,641	3,431,351	3,482,821
COGS	811,001	967,412	981,923	996,652	1,011,601
Gross Profit	1,927,223	2,298,908	2,398,718	2,434,699	2,471,220
Expenses					
Salary	54,000	54,810	55,632	56,467	57,314
Labor	720,336	741,946	764,204	787,131	810,745
Advertis.	90,000	90,900	91,809	92,727	93,654

Office Expenses	10,988	13,195	13,327	13,460	13,595
Rent	180,000	180,000	180,000	180,000	180,000
Utilities	22,258	26,729	26,996	27,266	27,538
Legal / Accoun	3,000	3,030	3,060	3,091	3,122
Insurance	4,800	4,848	4,896	4,945	4,995
Deprec.	140,000	237,500	168,150	124,020	117,090
Other	7,800	7,878	7,957	8,036	8,117
Total Expenses	1,233,182	1,360,836	1,316,032	1,297,143	1,316,169
EBIT	694,041	938,073	1,082,686	1,137,556	1,155,050
Interest Expense	34,758	34,205	33,612	32,976	32,294
Earnings before taxes	659,283	903,868	1,049,074	1,104,580	1,122,756
Taxes	131,857	180,774	209,815	220,916	224,551
Net Income	527,426	723,094	839,260	883,664	898,205

Analysis:

I started with the quarterly expected profit and loss projections that we calculated in the 12-month profit and loss section. Next, I added together the quarterly projections to come up with the first-year income statement projection. Once this was completed, I used the growth rates discussed in the growth rate section to project the next four years profit and losses in the income statement.

Balance Sheet:

The balance sheet is, for the most part, not absolutely needed in the business plan. This is because the projections for balance sheet will almost always be significantly off as compared to actual results. However, for the diehard entrepreneurs looking to cover all aspects of their financial expectations, presented below is a sample balance sheet.

Business Plan Writing Tip:

When discussing the balance sheet, make sure to explicitly state that the projections for the financial statement may change based on sales, operations, and other business needs. I like to put the statement before the balance sheet because of the significant fluctuation between projected returns and the actual results in the balance sheet.

When discussing the balance sheet, make sure to highlight the cash position and retained earnings. The cash position is important because this will show the reader that you, as the owner, expect to have enough liquid assets to operate the restaurant for the short and long term. As for the retained earnings, this section is where your net profit, minus dividends paid, ties into your balance sheet.

If your retained earnings grow at the same pace as your net profits, then this shows that your restaurant reinvests most of the profits earned. However, if the segment grows at a significantly slower pace as compared to your net income, then investors and bankers may ascertain that significant amount of your net profits are being paid out to the founder as dividends or other owners.

Sample:

Balance Sheet - Pro Forma					
Assets	Year 1	Year 2	Year 3	Year 4	Year 5
Cash	867,202	1,821,416	2,821,905	3,822,085	4,830,119
Accts Receiv.	-	-	-	-	-

Inventories	67,583	80,618	81,827	83,054	84,300
Total Curr. Assets	934,785	1,902,034	2,903,732	3,905,139	4,914,419
PP&E	1,360,000	1,360,000	1,360,000	1,360,000	1,360,000
Less Deprec.	140,000	377,500	545,650	669,670	786,760
Net PP&E	1,220,000	982,500	814,350	690,330	573,240
Total Assets	2,154,785	2,884,534	3,718,082	4,595,469	5,487,659

Balance Sheet - Pro Forma					
Liabilities	**Year 1**	**Year 2**	**Year 3**	**Year 4**	**Year 5**
Accounts Pay	67,583	80,618	81,827	83,054	84,300
Notes Payable	2,896	2,850	2,801	2,748	2,691
Accruals	64,528	66,396	68,320	70,300	72,338
Total Current Liab.	135,008	149,864	152,948	156,102	159,329
Loans	492,351	484,149	475,354	465,923	456,681
Total Liabilities	627,359	634,013	628,302	622,025	616,010
Common Stock	1,000,000	1,000,000	1,000,000	1,000,000	1,000,000
Retained Earnings	527,426	1,250,521	2,089,780	2,973,444	3,871,649
Total Com. Equity	1,527,426	2,250,521	3,089,780	3,973,444	4,871,649
Total Liab & Equity	2,154,785	2,884,534	3,718,082	4,595,469	5,487,659

Analysis:

In the example above, the restaurant owner can see that the retained earnings section of the balance sheet grows significantly year-over-year. This shows that the owner intends to reinvest a significant portion of their net profits back into the restaurant. By doing this, the restaurant owner increases the likelihood of success in the business.

Further, the example above showed the cash position grown significantly over a five-year time span. This also helps the restaurant owner show that they fully expect enough liquidity to support operations for the short and long term.

Financial Ratios:

Financial ratios utilize a restaurant's financial projections to show how efficient or profitable and organization will be based on the owner's best estimate. Common financial ratios include:

- Return on equity
- Return on assets
- Current ratio
- Profit margin

Return on Equity - Almost all investors are crazy about return on equity. This is because the return on equity indicates to investors how much the restaurant profited in relations to equity invested. As shown below, the calculation for return on equity is net income divided by total equity. Investors want to see this ratio as high as possible and climbing, over time. This is because either a restaurant is increasing its net income by using the same amount of equity invested or the firm is using less equity to generate the same amount of money.

Formula:

$$ROE = Net\ Income\ /\ Total\ Equity$$

Return on Assets - In keeping with the profitability thing, the return on assets allows investors to assess how profitable our target organization is as compared to the total assets utilized by the organization. With this ratio, investors prefer to see a relatively high return on assets. This indicates that the organization is generating net profits from assets as a whole.

Formula:

$$ROA = Net\ Income\ /\ Total\ Assets$$

Current Ratio - One of the most popular financial ratios is the current ratio. The current ratio measures the amount of cash inflow (money coming into the restaurant) over the last 12-months with the amount of cash outflow (bills that needed to be paid by the restaurant). From this measurement, we can determine whether the restaurant had enough money coming in to cover funds going out.

Formula:

$$Current\ Ratio = Current\ Assets\ /\ Current\ Liabilities$$

In the above formula, we can see that if a restaurant has more current assets than current liabilities, the answer will always be greater than one. However, if a restaurant has more current liabilities as compared to current assets, then the answer is going to be less than one.

Profit Margin - My personal favorite financial ratio is the profit margin. The profit margin ratio compares a restaurant's net income, or profits, with their revenues. Again, the higher this ratio, the better for investors. A distressing trend to be cognizant of, as an investor, is when the profit margin increases when revenues fall. This happens because management has taken it upon themselves to significantly cut costs within the restaurant. Unfortunately, this type of action is not sustainable. Further, cost-cutting often leads to long-term revenue decline.

Formula:

$$Profit\ Margin = Net\ Income\ /\ Total\ Revenues$$

Business Plan Writing Tip:

When writing the financial ratio section of the business plan, don't just provide the ratios, make sure to explain what the ratios actually mean. By doing this, the entrepreneur adds credibility to the calculations. Also, this will help show the importance of the ratios selected.

Sample:

Financial Ratios					
	Year 1	Year 2	Year 3	Year 4	Year 5
Return on Equity	34.53%	32.13%	27.16%	22.24%	18.44%
Return on Asset	24.48%	25.07%	22.57%	19.23%	16.37%
Current Ratio	6.92	12.69	18.99	25.02	30.84
Profit Margin	19.26%	22.14%	24.83%	25.75%	25.79%
Net Present Value	9,050,885				
IRR	83.40%				

Analysis:

In the sample above, the business owner expected to provide investors with a return on equity in the first year of 34.5%. As the organization grows, the return on equity is expected to decrease. Usually, this situation happens when the business owner continually reinvests their net profits. In other words, the business owner intends to utilize equity for growth opportunities as compared to taking on debt.

For the return on assets, the business owner in the scenario anticipates a 24.4% return on assets for the first year. This is anticipated to decline to 16.3% in year five. The reduction in return on assets may be partly due to holding a significant amount of cash. From the perspective of an investor, this may be of a minor concern because the excessive cash holding may be preferable than taking on additional risk for a startup restaurant.

As for the current ratio, this shows that the business intends to have a significant cash position in the first year and grow this position for the next several years. As a result, the business owner will have more than enough current assets to pay for their current liabilities.

As for the profit margin, this also is projected to increase. Specifically, the profit margin is anticipated to grow from 19.26% in year 1 to 25.79% in year 5. This indicates that the business owner expects revenues to increase at a faster pace than the cost of goods and fixed costs.

Step 8 – Funding Request

The funding request section should include four important components, which are potential funding sources, funding terms, use of funds, and fund repayment.

Sample:

Funding Request

To start operations, funding of $1,500,000 in debt or equity from a bank or investor is required. Debt funding is expected to have a term of 15 to 20 years with an interest rate between 8% to 10%. Principle and interest payments will be made monthly, using profits from the business. For investors, a negotiated percentage of ownership in the restaurant will be offered. In addition, after the second year of profitability, investors will be compensated through semi-annually dividend payments from business cash flows.

Received funds will be used as follows:

Startup Costs	
Category	**Estimate**
Equity Investment	1,000,000.00
Loan	500,000.00
Initial Build Out	900,000
Working Capital	125,000.00
Section: Equipment	
Restaurant Equipment (General)	75,000.00
FOH Equipment	35,000.00
BOH Equipment	40,000.00
Sub Total	150,000.00
Section: Operations	

Inventory	95,000.00
Supplies	150,000.00
Décor	28,000.00
Sub Total	273,000.00
Section: Office Equipment	
Office Equipment	25,000.00
Furniture	12,000.00
Sub Total	37,000.00
Section: Other	
Misc. Licenses	15,000.00
Sub Total	15,000.00
Total	**1,500,000.00**

Potential Funding Sources:

The potential funding source, or sources, are all of the channels that the restaurant owner may use to obtain funding for their organization. Popular funding sources include lending institutions, such as banks, private investors, and grants. Most recently, crowdfunding has become a popular source of financing as well.

Business Plan Writing Tip:

Make sure to discuss every source that may be consider for funding. Common sources include investors and lending institutions, such as banks or credit unions. However, other funding sources are available, as well. These may include grants or crowdfunding opportunities.

Sample:

To start operations, funding of $1,500,000 in debt or equity from a bank or investor is required.

Analysis:

As shown in the example above, for this restaurant owner, lending sources are limited to investors and lending institutions. If the owner decided to explore grants or crowdfunding opportunities, then the business plan should be updated to reflect these aspirations.

Funding Terms:

Funding terms are the range of terms that the restaurant owner will entertain. Funding terms may include a range of interest rates that would be acceptable to the owner for a loan. As for investors, terms with this party is a little bit more complicated. From this, just stating that an equity position is negotiable often will suffice.

Business Plan Writing Tip:

In the funding term section, make sure to tell the potential lender or investor your expectations or parameters for funding. These parameters should include a dollar amount for the loan or equity investment, length of time for loan, expected interest rate, or offer for a percentage of the restaurant to potential investors.

Sample:

Debt funding is expected to have a term of 15 to 20 years with an interest rate between 8% to 10%.

And

For investors, a negotiated percentage of ownership in the restaurant will be offered.

Analysis:

The dollar amount expected, or need is $1.5 million. For this particular segment, a specific dollar amount is highly recommended. However, in certain situations, a range of funding may be acceptable. Just make sure to explain why the range of funds is needed.

The second part is related to the term expected for the loan, which is between 15 and 20 years. For most other instances of the business funding request, ranges are more than acceptable; they are actually recommended to be honest.

Use of Funds:

The use of funds section is where the restauran owner shows the investor or lender where their money will be spent. Common use of funds includes working capital, which is money needed for general operations, buildout of a facility, if you need to rent an office space or retail space, and purchasing inventory.

Business Plan Writing Tip:

When I write a use of funds section, I always put the information in a spreadsheet and show a total at the bottom. Further, when categorizing the use of funds, try to use broad categories, such as office equipment, storage equipment, etc. By staying general with the categories, this allows the restaurant owner to use the funds as needed, but within the general budget.

Sample:

Startup Costs	
Category	**Estimate**
Equity Investment	1,000,000.00
Loan	500,000.00
Initial Build Out	900,000
Working Capital	125,000.00
Section: Equipment	
Restaurant Equipment (General)	75,000.00

FOH Equipment	35,000.00
BOH Equipment	40,000.00
Sub Total	150,000.00
Section: Operations	
Inventory	95,000.00
Supplies	150,000.00
Décor	28,000.00
Sub Total	273,000.00
Section: Office Equipment	
Office Equipment	25,000.00
Furniture	12,000.00
Sub Total	37,000.00
Section: Other	
Misc. Licenses	15,000.00
Sub Total	15,000.00
Total	**1,500,000.00**

Analysis:

In the example provided, my use of funds section is broken into segments to help with budgeting purposes. The segment utilized were equipment, operations, and office equipment. Further, in the structure provided, I also offer some totals for each segment. Not only does this show a well-thought-out startup funding structure, but this also helps the investor or loan officer ascertain whether some of the budgetary segments are in line with expectations.

Fund Repayment:

The fund repayment section will tell the investor or loan officer/underwriter how the loan or equity investment will be rewarded. For the most part, dividends and loan payments will be paid from profits in the restaurant. This may seem like common sense to you and me. However, surprisingly enough, some people actually pay funds from other businesses or even from retirement accounts. By explaining how the funds will be repaid, the investor or loan officer will have a full picture of how their investment will be compensated.

Business Plan Writing Tip:

When writing this section, I prefer to have the fund repayment information addressed in the final paragraph. This allows the investing parties to understand the totality of the funds situation before being introduced to the repayment segment.

Sample:

Principle and interest payments will be made monthly, using profits from the business. For investors, a negotiated percentage of ownership in the restaurant will be offered. In addition, after the second year of profitability, investors will be compensated through semi-annually dividend payments from business cash flows.

Analysis:

In the example provided, funds used to repay vested parties is clearly stated in the funding request. Further, principal and interest payments come from profits in the restaurant on a monthly basis. As for investors, their compensation will also come from cash flow in the restaurant, but only after the second-year of profitability.

Step 9 – Executive Summary

The executive summary is the first section that a business owner should present to the interested party. When I write my executive summaries, they are always an abbreviated version of the business plan. By doing this, essentially, a business owner has two documents. The first document may be considered an executive summary. This will briefly explain, in broad terms, what the restaurant is about, the menu items offered, differentiated items provided, financial outlook, and funds needed to start operations or grow the restaurant.

Restaurant and Product:

The restaurant and product section should briefly summarize the restaurant and menu items being offered.

Business Plan Writing Tip:

When I write this section, I will always copy and paste my restaurant summary and product description under the heading for the executive summary. Next, I literally just start deleting lines to reduce the content to approximately a paragraph.

For the second paragraph, I will then summarize the rest of the restaurant description section of the business plan, such as competitive advantage, hours of operation, number of employees, and any other critical pieces of information that I to show upfront about the restaurant.

Sample:

XYZ Restaurant is a limited liability restaurant located in Orlando, Florida. Our firm offers a Southern style menu offering for both breakfast and lunch. Our restaurant specializes in high-quality entrees in a downhome ambiance.

Our restaurant uses the best value pricing model to ensure a competitive price is offered to our customers. Our hours of operation are from 6:00 AM to 3 PM, seven days a week. Our staff size is four, including the owner. An important key to success in sustaining our business is to continually engage our target market through innovative advertising messages.

Analysis:

In the first paragraph, the location of the establishment, menu items, and differentiating factors are almost always discussed. This immediately shows the type of restaurant and how it is different from other restaurants in the area.

As for the second paragraph, this is always a summary of the rest of the information in the restaurant description. I like include the hours of operation, staff size, and how the restaurant will sustain operations in the long term.

Target Market:

The target market, as noted earlier in the book, is a demographic or group of individuals that may frequently visit our restaurant.

Business Plan Writing Tip:

For this section, I just simply note the target market and eliminate any additional information as to why the selection was made.

Sample:

Our primary target market will be young blue color works, specifically females between the ages of 25 to 35.

Analysis:

The sample tells shows the type of worker, age bracket, and gender of our target market and nothing more.

Financial Highlights:

The financial highlights section of the executive summary should stay focused on how the restaurant will perform, financially, over the next 12-months. Because of this limited focus, popular inclusions in the financial highlight summary section would be related to first-year annual profits, expenses aligned with these prophets, and net profits expected.

Business Plan Writing Tip:

I like to keep this section to approximately four lines. Further, I always first introduce the revenues and then the cost aligned with the revenues. With this done, I finished the paragraph with net profits and the profit margin ratio. The succinct financial summary shows investor or loan officer the restaurant's potential profits in short order.

Sample:

The financial projections are based on market research and empirical examination of the local restaurant industry. For the next year, we project revenues of approximately $456,793. The estimated expense costs will be $217,330. After taxes, we estimate a net profit of $239,463. This leads to a profit margin of approximately 52.4%.

Analysis:

The summarized version of the financial summary is definitely short and sweet. The most important aspects of the financial statements are included in the short paragraph. Further, the structure of the financial summary almost tells a story. First, it starts with revenues, then shows the cost involved with the revenues. Once the costs are deducted, then the profits are shown. Finally, a real quick ratio was presented, as well.

Funding:

Differing from the other sections in the executive summary, the funding section should be almost identical to the funding section in the business plan, with the exception of the cost breakdown. Not surprisingly, investors want to know how much money the restaurant needs and how the they will be repaid. There is no skimping on details here.

Business Plan Writing Tip:

The section should be written in terms similar to, or identical to, the funding section of the business plan, as noted above.

Sample:

To start operations, funding of $1,500,000 in debt or equity from a bank or investor is required. Debt funding is expected to have a term of 15 to 20 years with an interest rate between 8% to 10%. Principle and interest payments will be made monthly, using profits from the restaurant. For investors, a negotiated percentage of ownership in the restaurant will be offered. In addition, after the second year of profitability, investors will be compensated through semi-annually dividend payments from business cash flows.

Analysis:

Not much need for analysis. Just copy and paste and ignore the startup cost. You are now ready to go.

Step 10 – Appendix

The appendix section is used for charts, graphs, and other documents that support the business plan.

Resumes:

For almost all business plans, I will include the restaurant owner's resume in the appendix section. The resume helps to support experiences noted in the management and organization section of the business plan.

Business Plan Writing Tip:

When including a resume in a business plan, stay away from the pictures and fancy fonts. Usually, the reader is more interested in understanding the restaurant owners' experiences and education related to the proposed business.

Sample:

Paul Borosky

XXX Rachelle Dr. Apt XXX - Sanford, FL. 32771 - (321) 948-**** –
Paulb@Qualitybusinessplan.com

Professional Experience

Quality Business Plan
Plan Writing
Sanford, Fl. / Online
October, 2010 - Present

Business Consulting – Business

* Prepared pro forma financial statements.

* Research various industries for trends, revenues, and growth projections.

* Calculate various financial ratios such as Return on Equity and Current Ratio.

* Write business plans for current and prospective businesses.

XXX High school   **Entrepreneurship / Microsoft Office / Computer Programming Instructor**

Durham, NC.   * Prepare lesson plans for Excel, Word, Visual Basic, and other classes.

August, 2014 – October, 2016   * Assign and grade various assignments.

* Provide in-depth student feedback in residential settings.

* Assist students through numerous stages of learning.

XXX College   **Resident and Online Adjunct Finance / Entrepreneurship Instructor**

Ocala, Fl.   * Prepare lesson plans for residential class.

June, 2013 – December 2016   * Assign and grade various finance assignments.

* Provide in-depth student feedback in residential and online settings.

* Assist students through numerous stages of learning.

* Subject Matter Expert – Created and Designed college level finance classes.

Walt Disney World Resorts Supervisor   **Quick Service Food -**

Orlando, Fl.   * Prepared guest meals in fast pace environment.

April, 2011-Jan, 2013   * Display exceptional customer service to guest.

* Daily practice Disney's leader basics.

* Lead other cast members by example and instruction.

Education

Northcentral University   DBA, Management – Doctoral Candidate Ongoing

Webster University   Finance – 21 Master level credit hours 2011

Webster University (MBA)	Masters in Business Administration 2010
Barry University	Bachelors in Professional Studies with specialization in Administration 2009
Seminole State College	AA Degree 2002

Training and Skills

Blackboard Learning System	Rasmussen College 2016
Microsoft PowerPoint Certified	Certiport 2016
Microsoft Excel Certified	Certiport 2016
Microsoft Word Certified	Certiport 2015
Canvas Learning System	Voyager High School 2015
NC Department of Education License	Temporary Professional Educator's 2014
Angel Learning System	Rasmussen College 2013
Fl. Department of Education Business (grades 6-12)	Statement of Status of Eligibility – 2013
Online Faculty Training	Rasmussen College 2013
Salesforce	Training for Salesforce software 2013

Analysis:

In this example, the proposed restaurant owner starts off by highlighting the professional experiences. In some cases, educational experiences may come first. The decision really depends on where the most experience lies. If the owner has significant work experience, then go with professional experiences first. However, if education better supports the restaurant concept, then, by all means, rearrange your resume to lead off with education. A final analysis note would be that there is no variation in colors, fancy fonts, or other tactics to spruce up the resume design. Always keep in mind, the star of the show is a restaurant and not the owner.

Summary

In summary, the restaurant business plan writing process is definitely long, tedious, and detailed, to say the least. However, by following the discussed business plan writing process in this book AND by using the sample and template provided, you now have the tools and training to complete you very own restaurant business plan!

Best of luck with your endeavor!

Restaurant Business Plan Sample

Executive Summary

Restaurant Summary: XYZ Restaurant is a limited liability restaurant located in Orlando, Florida. Our firm offers a Southern style menu offering for both breakfast and lunch. Our restaurant specializes in high-quality entrees in a downhome ambiance.

Our restaurant uses the best value pricing model to ensure a competitive price is offered to our customers. Our hours of operation are from 6:00 AM to 3 PM, seven days a week. Our staff size is four, including the owner. An important key to success in sustaining our business is to continually engage our target market through innovative advertising messages.

Target Market: Our primary target market will be young blue color works, specifically females between the ages of 25 to 35.

Financial Highlights: The financial projections are based on market research and empirical examination of the local restaurant industry. For the next year, we project revenues of approximately $456,793. The estimated expense costs will be $217,330. After taxes, we estimate a net profit of $239,463. This leads to a profit margin of approximately 52.4%.

Funding Request: To start operations, funding of $1,500,000 in debt or equity from a bank or investor is required. Debt funding is expected to have a term of 15 to 20 years with an interest rate between 8% to 10%. Principle and interest payments will be made monthly, using profits from the restaurant. For investors, a negotiated percentage of ownership in the restaurant will be offered. In addition, after the second year of profitability, investors will be compensated through semi-annually dividend payments from business cash flows.

Restaurant Description

Restaurant Summary

ABC Restaurant will be a limited liability corporation located at 123 Broadway St. in Orlando, FL. Our business owner(s) will be John Smith. Our casual dining breakfast restaurant will focus on popular breakfast menu items such as eggs with breakfast meats, pancakes, omelets, chicken and waffles, and more. As for a lunch menu, this includes popular sandwiches, burgers, and home-made soups. Our hours of operation will be from 6 AM To 2:30 PM, seven days a week.

Competitive Advantages

ABC Restaurant will have specific competitive advantages once our firm starts operations. First, our restaurant will use local, farm-fresh produce and dairy products when possible. No other restaurant in the area has committed to this business model. Further, our firm will embrace the "fusion" concept in our menu items. For our fusion concept, we will offer both popular Mexican dishes, as well as, down-home Southern meals as a building block for our restaurant.

Products/Services Description

Breakfast
Our breakfast menu items include omelets, pancakes, waffles, breakfast burritos, and Southern biscuits and gravy

Lunch:
For our lunch menu, we focus on sandwiches, soups, and burgers. Popular items include the "American Burger," topped with American cheese, lettuce, tomatoes, and pickles. Another popular lunch item will be our wide selection of soups.

Beverages:
Similar to other breakfast restaurants, we will offer traditional coffees, juices, and sodas.

For a full menu selection, please review Appendix A.

Pricing Strategy

Our pricing structure will be focused on the best value strategy. For this strategy, our management team will continually research prices of comparable food and drink menu items offered by local restaurant competitors in the area. From this research, we will create base menu item prices using the averages of competitors in the area. Next, our organization will make menu item price adjustments based on the quality of ingredients, the ambiance of the competitors' eateries, and overall menu selection as compared to ours. The end objective is to have all of our menu item prices competitively priced using the best value strategic model.

Business Models

Operations:
Our operational structure will seek to achieve a quick-service restaurant's speed of service while offering high-quality meals that would rival a casual dining experience. As a customer approaches our restaurant, they will be met with our menu posted on the door or chalkboard stand out front. This will allow visitors to decide upon their favorite dish before entering the restaurant.

At the counter, our customers will be able to point to and select food items for purchase. Once the selection process is complete, we cook the items and bring the food to the register for payment. In total, the process for each guest should be less than four minutes.

Hours of Operations:
Our hours of operations business model will be structured to ensure our restaurant customers' needs are met at a convenient time. From this, our organization will be open from 6 AM to 2:30 PM, seven days a week.

Location

As previously stated, our location will be in the Orlando, Florida area. The proposed location size will be about 4,500 square feet. Approximately three-quarters of the area will be dedicated to the front of the house operations. The rest of the area will be devoted to the back of the house operations, office space, and storage.

As for competition, this area has few other Southern breakfast restaurants within a several miles radius. This will enable us to capture a significant portion of the casual dining breakfast restaurant market share in the area.

Future Plans

Within the next 24 months, our firm will open new locations in the Orlando / Central Florida area. The new sites and timeframe will be based on funding, leadership availability, and other factors. Further, our management team will introduce new menu items within the next 12 months. These menu items will be selected based on customer demand, how well the menu item will complement our current offering, and availability of fresh ingredients.

Business Objectives and Time Line

1 - 3 Months
- o Obtain investor funding.
- o Identify facility and negotiate a rental agreement.
- o Engage in buildout activities.
- o Open for business.

3 – 6 Months
- o Start an advertising campaign.
- o Evaluate marketing strategy and implement.
- o Evaluate business models.

6 – 12 Months
- o Optimize marketing strategies.
- o Optimize business models.
- o Examine external environment for market opportunities.

Mission Statement

"Our restaurant's mission is to provide the best Southern-style entrées in a friendly atmosphere and clean environment."

Vision Statement

"Deliver world-class Southern breakfast delights on a global level."

Value Statement

- o   Honesty.
- o   Fair prices.
- o   High-quality dishes.
- o   Technical innovations

Keys to Success

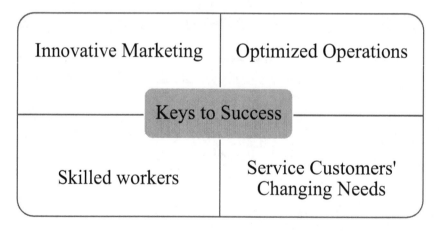

Target Market

Primary Target Market

Our primary target market will be young, blue color works. Specifically, females between the ages of 25 to 35. This demographic was selected because of their propensity to enjoy Southern breakfast cuisines while socializing with friends and family.

Secondary Target Market

As for the secondary target market, this will be medical professionals working at the hospital across the street or in medical facilities surrounding the hospital. This demographic was selected due to their proximity to our restaurant.

Target Market Growth

Based on research from website XYZ, the current blue color work force in ABC City is 250,000 people. The U.S. Census Bureau has noted that the city's population increased by 1.3% annually over the last five years. Based on this factor, our restaurant owner expects a similar growth rate for the next five years. From this, the target market formulation will be 253,250 within the next 12 months. In two years, our target market population will expand to 256,543 people.

Market Analysis

Industry Overview

Juice and smoothie bars sell fruit drinks, protein shakes, vegetable drinks, and other healthy food and drink items. The foodservice industry, as a whole, should exceed $5 billion next year. The juice and smoothie bars industry, which is a sub section of the foodservice industry, will reach over $3 billion in sales for 2019. For the next several years, industry experts project annual revenue growth of approximately 1.8%.

Industry Statistics

- Studies have shown that close to 30% of all US adults do not meet or exceed their daily servings of vegetables and fruit.
- On a global basis, juice bar sales have exceeded $9 billion.
- Premium juice sales have grown by approximately 11% since 2000.
- 83% of consumers have stated that a fruit-based smoothie is preferable as compared to a dairy base.

Threats, Trends, and Opportunities

An important threat to an industry would be related to the overall economy. Currently, job growth and employment are at all-time-highs. From this, people have enough discretionary funds to afford dining out. Unfortunately, in the event of an economic recession, as discretionary funds for people decrease, profits for the restaurant industry may show a correlated effect.

As for an opportunity, casual dinners are increasing selecting "mom and pop" restaurants over chain restaurants due to better service and appealing menu selections. This allows for startup restaurants to enter the market place and gain a loyal following. Finally, trends in the restaurant industry may be found in technological innovations. Technological innovations may help restaurant owners offer better-quality foods or enhanced service for premium prices.

Keys to Success

To be successful in the restaurant industry, competitors need to focus on hiring skilled employees. In other words, small businesses must employ and retain qualified and well-trained workers. Qualifications may not necessarily be in traditional schooling. However, experience with kitchen prep, serving, and hosting is necessitated to ensure that a guest has a memorable visit to a restaurant.

SWOT Analysis

Strengths
Management experience.
Documented plans
Themed restaurant
  concept
Training program

Weakness
Startup restaurant.
Untested business
  location.

Opportunities
Community involvement
Appeal to a wide variety
  of clientele.
Location
Brand building

Threats
Local competitors
Susceptible to
  economic downturn.

Competitive Analysis

Dine Here Restaurant is a "mom and pop" restaurant in the Washington DC. area. The restaurant was founded in 1984 and prides themselves on their 24hr availability. As for services, the diner offers a limited menu, focused on breakfast, lunch, and dinner. Based on a Google search, customers have had mixed reviews. Most reviews seemed satisfied with the diner's food quality and service. However, some past customers complained that the cleanliness of the facility was lacking.

Organization and Management

Management Summary

John Smith, Sr., MBA., is the founder and CEO of ABC Restaurant. He has started and managed numerous successful small restaurants over the last ten years. Restaurants started, and managed, includes a breakfast cafe, food truck, and 24-hour diner. For each business, he was responsible for all aspects of the organizations, from marketing to strategic planning.

Job Responsibilities

CEO:
- Create and execute marketing strategies for business growth.
- Align business strategies with the vision statement.
- Negotiating contracts with vendors.
- Ensure legal compliance for the business.
- Continually examine the firm's external environment for new market opportunities.

General Manager:
- Control inventory to ensure optimal levels are attained.
- Manage day-to-day operations of the restaurant.
- Servers and cooks during high volume times.
- Interview and hire new employees.
- Assist in the onboarding process for new employees.

Organizational Chart

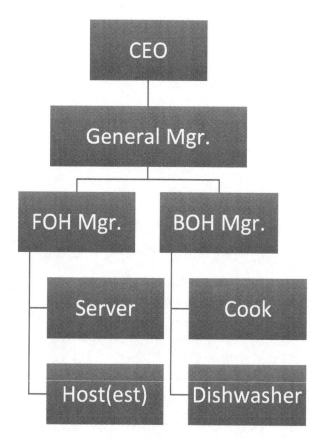

Marketing

Marketing Objectives and Keys to Success

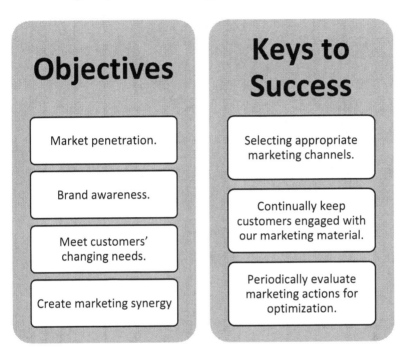

Traditional Marketing

Our first traditional marketing channel will include a professionally designed sign for the front of the restaurant. This sign will include our restaurant name, logo, and slogan. Further, prominent colors will include black, gold, and white. The objective of the signage is to let potential customers know our restaurant's theme and possible menu items offered.

Internet Marketing

The importance of a professionally designed website cannot be understated. To exploit this opportunity, XYZ Restaurant will create and maintain a website and Yelp listing. The objective for the strategy is to effectively communicate our restaurant's theme and highlight our menu items.

Social Media Marketing

ABC Restaurant's social media advertising will include Instagram, Twitter, and Facebook. Using a three-channel approach to social media will ensure our message reaches a broad audience, which will include our target market. In addition, several potential customers will receive an advertising message on multiple social media outlets. This should exceed the needed repetition of our message to a broad audience as well as our target market. The marketing message will focus on our restaurant menu items offered, and possible weekly specials.

Financial Projections

Financial Assumptions

Our financial projections have several assumptions based on research and management's expectation of potential sales and costs.

- All financial projections are based on management and or owner(s) professional expectations of sales and expenses for the foreseeable future.

- In the first 12 months, sales should increase by approximately 5% each month. In months 13 to 24, sales growth should slow to approximately .3% per month. For years three through five, sales are expected to grow by 4.5%.

- The cost of goods or variable costs are expected to be approximately 30.21% of total sales.

- The initial advertising budget will be $7,5000. Advertising is projected to increase by approximately 1% per year. This is to ensure maximum utilization of the firm's property and equipment.

- Cost projections were calculated using a common size model. This practice is typical for financial modeling.

- The tax rate was assumed to be 20%. Fluctuation in the tax rate will have a direct impact on net profits.

- Initial funding needed is 1,500,000. An increase/decrease in amount will impact the net present value and internal rate of return.

- Starting cash balance needed is $125,000 for working capital.

- Cash account was used to balance assets with liabilities and equity.

Financial Summary

The financial projections are based on market research and empirical examination of the local restaurant industry. For the next year, we project revenues of approximately $456,793. The estimated expense costs will be $217,330. After taxes, we estimate a net profit of $239,463. This leads to a profit margin of approximately 52.4%. As our brand continues to grow, second-year progression is anticipated to yield a net income of approximately $311,363. Within five years, net income should exceed $348,722.

Startup Costs

Startup Costs	
Category	Estimate
Equity Investment	1,000,000.00
Loan	500,000.00
Initial Build Out	900,000
Working Capital	125,000.00
Section: Equipment	
Restaurant Equipment (General)	75,000.00
FOH Equipment	35,000.00
BOH Equipment	40,000.00
Sub Total	150,000.00
Section: Operations	
Inventory	95,000.00
Supplies	150,000.00
Décor	28,000.00
Sub Total	273,000.00

Section: Office Equipment	
Office Equipment	25,000.00
Furniture	12,000.00
Sub Total	37,000.00
Section: Other	
Misc. Licenses	15,000.00
Sub Total	15,000.00
Total	1,500,000.00

Daily Revenues

Average Daily Sales							
Revenue Generators							
Daily Sales	% Sales	Num.	Price	Cost	Profit	Total Rev.	Total Cost
Breakfast Sand.	20%	90	9.50	1.90	7.60	855	171
Platters	20%	90	13.50	2.70	10.80	1,215	243
Other	20%	120	7.50	1.50	6.00	900	180
Lunch and Dinner Entrees	30%	165	14.50	4.35	10.15	2,392	717
Side items	50%	60	7.50	3.75	3.75	450	225
Other	50%	90	6.50	3.25	3.25	585	292
					Total	6,398	1,829

Labor

Labor				
Employee	Number	Rate	Monthly Hours	Total Pay
Salary		n/a	n/a	4,500
Manager	1	25.00	172	4,300
Employees	18	18.00	172	55,728
			Total	60,028

Monthly Fixed Costs

Monthly Fixed Costs	
Monthly Costs	Monthly Total
Rent	15,000
Utilities	1,580
Office Expenses	780
Insurance	400
Accounting/legal	250
Advertising	7500
Other	650
Monthly Total	26,160

Growth Rates

Growth Rates	
Growth Rate Sales 2 & 3	3.50%
Growth Rate Sales 4 & 5	1.50%
Growth Rate Cost of Goods	1.50%

Growth Rate Salary	1.50%
Growth Rate Labor	3.00%
Growth Advertising	1.00%
Growth Office	1.00%
Growth Utility	1.00%
Growth Legal	1.00%
Growth Insurance	1.00%
Growth Other	1.00%

Misc. Information

Misc. Information	
Tax Rate	20%
Cost of Capital	10%

Loan Payment Calculations

Loan Information	
Loan Amount	(500,000.00)
Interest Rate	7%
Term	25
Payment	$3,533.90

Profit and Loss Quarter 1

Pro Forma Income Statement Year 1 Quarter 1				
	Month 1	Month 2	Month 3	Quarter 1
Revenues	192,941	198,729	204,691	596,361
COGS	57,145	58,859	60,625	176,629
Gross Profit	135,796	139,870	144,066	419,732
Expenses				
Salary				

	4,500	4,500	4,500	13,500
Labor	60,028	60,028	60,028	180,084
Advertising	7,500	7,500	7,500	22,500
Office Expen.	780	803	828	2,411
Rent	15,000	15,000	15,000	45,000
Utilities	1,580	1,627	1,676	4,884
Legal / Account	250	250	250	750
Insurance	400	400	400	1,200
Depreciation	11,667	11,667	11,667	35,000
Other	650	650	650	1,950
Total Expenses	102,355	102,425	102,498	307,279
EBIT	33,441	37,445	41,568	112,454
Interest Expense	2,917	2,913	2,909	8,739
EBT	30,525	34,532	38,658	103,715
Taxes	6,105	6,906	7,732	20,743
Net Income	24,420	27,625	30,927	82,972

Profit and Loss Quarter 2

Pro Forma Income Statement Year 1 Quarter 2				
Income Statement	Month 4	Month 5	Month 6	Quarter 2
Revenues	210,832	217,157	223,671	651,660

COGS	62,444	64,317	66,247	193,007
Gross Profit	148,388	152,840	157,425	458,653
Expenses				
Salary	4,500	4,500	4,500	13,500
Labor	60,028	60,028	60,028	180,084
Advertising	7,500	7,500	7,500	22,500
Office Expen.	828	878	904	2,610
Rent	15,000	15,000	15,000	45,000
Utilities	1,676	1,778	1,832	5,286
Legal / Account	250	250	250	750
Insurance	400	400	400	1,200
Depreciation	11,667	11,667	11,667	35,000
Other	650	650	650	1,950
Total Expenses	102,498	102,651	102,731	307,880
EBIT	45,890	50,189	54,694	150,773
Interest Expense	2,906	2,902	2,898	8,706
EBT	42,984	47,287	51,796	142,067
Taxes	8,597	9,457	10,359	28,413
Net Income	34,387	37,829	41,437	113,653

Profit and Loss Quarter 3

Pro Forma Income Statement Year 1 Quarter 3				
Income Statement	Month 7	Month 8	Month 9	Quarter 3
Revenues	230,382	237,293	244,412	712,087
COGS	68,234	70,281	72,389	210,904
Gross Profit	162,148	167,012	172,022	501,182
Expenses				
Salary	4,500	4,500	4,500	13,500
Labor	60,028	60,028	60,028	180,084
Advertising	7,500	7,500	7,500	22,500
Office Expen.	904	959	988	2,852
Rent	15,000	15,000	15,000	45,000
Utilities	1,832	1,943	2,001	5,776
Legal / Account	250	250	250	750
Insurance	400	400	400	1,200
Depreciation	11,667	11,667	11,667	35,000
Other	650	650	650	1,950
Total Expenses	102,731	102,897	102,984	308,612
EBIT	59,417	64,115	69,038	192,570
Interest Expense	2,895	2,891	2,887	8,673

EBT	56,522	61,224	66,151	183,897
Taxes	11,304	12,245	13,230	36,779
Net Income	45,218	48,979	52,921	147,118

Profit and Loss Quarter 4

Pro Forma Income Statement Year 1 Quarter 4				
Income Statement	Month 10	Month 11	Month 12	Quarter 4
Revenues	251,744	259,297	267,075	778,116
COGS	74,561	76,798	79,102	230,461
Gross Profit	177,183	182,499	187,974	547,655
Expenses				
Salary	4,500	4,500	4,500	13,500
Labor	60,028	60,028	60,028	180,084
Advertising	7,500	7,500	7,500	22,500
Office Expen.	988	1,048	1,080	3,116
Rent	15,000	15,000	15,000	45,000
Utilities	2,001	2,123	2,187	6,312
Legal / Account	250	250	250	750
Insurance	400	400	400	1,200
Depreciation	11,667	11,667	11,667	35,000
Other	650	650	650	1,950

Total Expenses	102,984	103,166	103,261	309,412
EBIT	74,199	79,332	84,712	238,243
Interest Expense	2,883	2,880	2,876	8,639
EBT	71,315	76,453	81,836	229,604
Taxes	14,263	15,291	16,367	45,921
Net Income	57,052	61,162	65,469	183,684

Income Statement

Pro Forma Income Statement - Base					
	Year 1	Year 2	Year 3	Year 4	Year 5
Revenues	2,738,224	3,266,320	3,380,641	3,431,351	3,482,821
COGS	811,001	967,412	981,923	996,652	1,011,601
Gross Profit	1,927,223	2,298,908	2,398,718	2,434,699	2,471,220
Expenses					
Salary	54,000	54,810	55,632	56,467	57,314
Labor	720,336	741,946	764,204	787,131	810,745
Advert.	90,000	90,900	91,809	92,727	93,654
Office Expenses	10,988	13,195	13,327	13,460	13,595
Rent	180,000	180,000	180,000	180,000	180,000
Utilities	22,258	26,729	26,996	27,266	27,538
Legal / Account	3,000	3,030	3,060	3,091	3,122

Insur.	4,800	4,848	4,896	4,945	4,995
Deprec.	140,000	237,500	168,150	124,020	117,090
Other	7,800	7,878	7,957	8,036	8,117
Total Expenses	1,233,182	1,360,836	1,316,032	1,297,143	1,316,169
EBIT	694,041	938,073	1,082,686	1,137,556	1,155,050
Interest Expense	34,758	34,205	33,612	32,976	32,294
Earnings before taxes	659,283	903,868	1,049,074	1,104,580	1,122,756
Taxes	131,857	180,774	209,815	220,916	224,551
Net Income	527,426	723,094	839,260	883,664	898,205

Balance Sheet

Balance Sheet - Pro Forma					
Assets	**Year 1**	**Year 2**	**Year 3**	**Year 4**	**Year 5**
Cash	867,202	1,821,416	2,821,905	3,822,085	4,830,119
Accts Receiv.	-	-	-	-	-
Invent.	67,583	80,618	81,827	83,054	84,300
Total Curr. Assets	934,785	1,902,034	2,903,732	3,905,139	4,914,419
PP&E	1,360,000	1,360,000	1,360,000	1,360,000	1,360,000
Less Deprec.	140,000	377,500	545,650	669,670	786,760

Net PP&E	1,220,000	982,500	814,350	690,330	573,240
Total Assets	2,154,785	2,884,534	3,718,082	4,595,469	5,487,659

Balance Sheet - Pro Forma					
Liabilities	Year 1	Year 2	Year 3	Year 4	Year 5
Accounts Pay	67,583	80,618	81,827	83,054	84,300
Notes Payable	2,896	2,850	2,801	2,748	2,691
Accruals	64,528	66,396	68,320	70,300	72,338
Total Current Liab.	135,008	149,864	152,948	156,102	159,329
Loans	492,351	484,149	475,354	465,923	456,681
Total Liab.	627,359	634,013	628,302	622,025	616,010
Common Stock	1,000,000	1,000,000	1,000,000	1,000,000	1,000,000
Retained Earnings	527,426	1,250,521	2,089,780	2,973,444	3,871,649
Total Com. Equity	1,527,426	2,250,521	3,089,780	3,973,444	4,871,649
Total Liab & Equity	2,154,785	2,884,534	3,718,082	4,595,469	5,487,659

Financial Ratios

Financial Ratios					
	Year 1	Year 2	Year 3	Year 4	Year 5
Return on Equity	34.53%	32.13%	27.16%	22.24%	18.44%
Return on Asset	24.48%	25.07%	22.57%	19.23%	16.37%
Current					

Ratio	6.92	12.69	18.99	25.02	30.84
Profit Margin	19.26%	22.14%	24.83%	25.75%	25.79%
Net Present Value	9,050,885				
IRR	83.40%				

Funding Request

To start operations, funding of $1,500,000 in debt or equity from a bank or investor is required. Debt funding is expected to have a term of 15 to 20 years with an interest rate between 8% to 10%. Principle and interest payments will be made monthly, using profits from the business. For investors, a negotiated percentage of ownership in the restaurant will be offered. In addition, after the second year of profitability, investors will be compensated through semi-annually dividend payments from business cash flows.

Received funds will be used as follows:

Startup Costs	
Category	**Estimate**
Equity Investment	1,000,000.00
Loan	500,000.00
Initial Build Out	900,000
Working Capital	125,000.00
Section: Equipment	
Restaurant Equipment (General)	75,000.00
FOH Equipment	35,000.00
BOH Equipment	40,000.00
Sub Total	150,000.00
Section: Operations	
Inventory	95,000.00
Supplies	150,000.00
Décor	28,000.00
Sub Total	273,000.00
Section: Office Equipment	
Office Equipment	25,000.00

Furniture	12,000.00
Sub Total	37,000.00
Section: Other	
Misc. Licenses	15,000.00
Sub Total	15,000.00
Total	**1,500,000.00**

Paul Borosky

XXX Rachelle Dr. - Sanford, FL. 32771 - (321) 948-**** –
Paulb@Qualitybusinessplan.com

Professional Experience

Quality Business Plan
Plan Writing
Sanford, Fl. / Online
October, 2010 - Present

Business Consulting – Business

* Prepared pro forma financial statements.
* Research various industries for trends, revenues, and growth projections.
* Calculate various financial ratios such as Return on Equity and Current Ratio.
* Write business plans for current and prospective businesses.

XXX High school
Office / Computer Programming Instructor
Durham, NC.
August, 2014 – October, 2016

Entrepreneurship / Microsoft

* Prepare lesson plans for Excel, Word, Visual Basic, and other classes.
* Assign and grade various assignments.
* Provide in-depth student feedback in residential settings.
* Assist students through numerous stages of learning.

XXX College
Finance / Entrepreneurship Instructor
Ocala, Fl.
June, 2013 – December 2016

Resident and Online Adjunct

* Prepare lesson plans for residential class.
* Assign and grade various finance assignments.
* Provide in-depth student feedback in residential and online settings.
* Assist students through numerous stages of learning.

* Subject Matter Expert – Created and Designed college level finance classes.

Walt Disney World Resorts Supervisor
Orlando, Fl.
April, 2011-Jan, 2013

Quick Service Food -

* Prepared guest meals in fast pace environment.

* Display exceptional customer service to guest.

* Daily practice Disney's leader basics.

* Lead other cast members by example and instruction.

Education

Northcentral University	DBA, Management – Doctoral Candidate Ongoing
Webster University	Finance – 21 Master level credit hours 2011
Webster University (MBA)	Masters in Business Administration 2010
Barry University	Bachelors in Professional Studies with specialization in Administration 2009
Seminole State College	AA Degree 2002

Training and Skills

Blackboard Learning System	Rasmussen College 2016
Microsoft PowerPoint Certified	Certiport 2016
Microsoft Excel Certified	Certiport 2016
Microsoft Word Certified	Certiport 2015
Canvas Learning System	Voyager High School 2015
NC Department of Education License	Temporary Professional Educator's 2014

Angel Learning System	Rasmussen College
	2013
Fl. Department of Education Business (grades 6-12)	Statement of Status of Eligibility – 2013
Online Faculty Training	Rasmussen College
	2013
Salesforce	Training for Salesforce software

Restaurant Business Plan Template (Includes Market Research!)

Executive Summary

Restaurant Summary: (Restaurant Name) is a (Business legal structure: limited liability corporation, sole proprietor, corporation) located in City, State. Our firm offers (product and services offered).

Our (type of restaurant: casual dining, café, quick service) business specializes in (what will your restaurant do best?).

(Name of restaurant) utilizes a (pricing strategy: best value, low price, premium) pricing model to ensure a fair price is offered to our customers. Our hours of operation are from (8:00 AM to 10 PM), (seven days a week, Monday – Friday, etc.). Our staff size is (four), including the owner. An important key to success in sustaining our restaurant is to (important action that your restaurant needs to take in order to succeed).

Target Market: Our primary target market will be (expected target market) between the ages of (age) to (age).

Financial Highlights: The financial projections are based on market research and empirical examination of the local restaurant industry. For the next year, we project revenues of approximately $(dollar amount). The estimated expense costs will be $(dollar amount). After taxes, we estimate a net profit of $(dollar amount). This leads to a profit margin of approximately (percent)%.

Funding Request: To start operations, funding of $(dollar amount) in debt or equity from a bank or investor is required. Debt funding is expected to have a term of (15) to (20) years with an interest rate between (rate)% to (rate)%. Principle and interest payments will be made monthly, using profits from the business. For investors, a negotiated percentage of ownership in the restaurant will be offered. In addition, investors will be compensated through (when will dividends be paid: quarterly, semi-annually, etc.) dividend payments from business cash flows.

Restaurant Description

Restaurant Summary

(Restaurant Name) will be a (business legal structure: corporate, sole proprietor, limited liability corporation, corporate, etc.) located at (address) in (city, state). Business owner will be (your name). Our (type of restaurant: café, casual dining, etc.) will offer on (menu items offered offered). Our hours of operation will be from (hours of operations).

Competitive Advantages

(Name of Restaurant) will have specific competitive advantages once our firm starts operations. First, (your main competitive advantage).

A second competitive advantage would be (second competitive advantage).

Menu Description

(Menu item 1)
Our (*Menu item 1*) will (describe menu item? What ingredients will be used?).

(Menu item 2)
Our (*Menu item 2*) will (describe menu item? What ingredients will be used?).

(Menu item 3)
Our (*Menu item 3*) will (describe menu item? What ingredients will be used?).

Pricing Strategy

Our pricing structure will be focused on a (low cost, best value, premium) pricing. The strategy was selected because (explain why you selected this pricing strategy).

Business Models

Operations:

Our operational structure will (describe how your restaurant will operate).

Hours of Operations:

Our hours of operations business model will be structured to ensure our customers' needs are met at a convenient time. From this, our organization will be open from (hours of operation).

Location

As previously stated, our location will be at (restaurant address). The proposed location size will be about (number) square feet. Approximately (percent) of the area will be dedicated to (what will be the main use of your facility). The rest of the area will be dedicated to (what else will your location be used for?).

As for competition, this area has about (number) competitors, offering similar menu items within a (number) square mile range.

Future Plans

Within the next (number) months, our firm will (discuss your future plans).

Business Objectives and Time Line

1 - 3 Months

- o Objective 1
- o Objective 2
- o Objective 3
- o Objective 4

3 – 6 Months

- o Objective 1
- o Objective 2
- o Objective 3

6 – 12 Months

- o Objective 1
- o Objective 2
- o Objective 3

Mission Statement

(Enter your mission statement here)

Vision Statement

(Enter your vision statement here)

Value Statement

- o Value 1
- o Value 2
- o Value 3
- o Value 4

Keys to Success

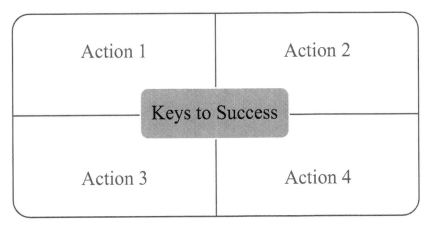

Target Market

Primary Target Market

Our primary target market will be (describe target market), specifically (male or female) between the ages of (age) to (age). This demographic was selected because (talk about why you selected this target market).

Secondary Target Market

As for secondary target market, this will be (describe target market), specifically (male or female) between the ages of (age) to (age). This demographic was selected because (talk about why you selected this target market).

Target Market Growth

Based on research from (where did you get the target market growth information), the current target market population in the area is about (number) (individuals or businesses).

The (name of source for researched information) has noted that the city's population has increased by (percent)% annually over the last (number) years. Based on this factor, our restaurant expects a similar growth rate for the next (number) years. From this, the target market formulation will be (number) within the next (number) months. In two years, our target market population will expand to (number) (people or businesses).

Restaurant Market Analysis

In this market analysis, the industry, economy and overall risk for the company will be analyzed for a better understanding of our external environment.

Industry: Restaurant Industry.

The restaurant industry is immensely popular in the US. Total sales for the industry in 2018 were about 825 billion[1]. These sales were generated from over 1 million establishments. Multinational corporations account for a large portion of sales. However, single unit owners capture the numerous niche markets in the industry. This has led to 7 in every 10 restaurants opened are single unit owner[2]. From this review, entrepreneurs with a creative twist to operating a restaurant may carve out significant revenues from the industry.

Growth:

Over the last five years, the restaurant industry has experienced approximately 3.7% growth annually[3]. Future growth in the restaurant industry is expected to be approximately 5.1% annually, which is adjusted for inflation[2].

Trends:

Growth in the restaurant industry has been steady for the last several years. However, recently, several chain restaurant operators have

---

[1] https://www.fesmag.com/features/foodservice-news/16150-foodservice-industry-forecast-for-2019-steady-state
[2] www.Restaurant.org.

experienced above normal increased revenues. An important segment of this growth is delivery and take-out orders. This is noteworthy because delivery and takeout orders require less work from staff.

Threats:

The restaurant industry does has specific threats. As the economy continues to grow, the labor market will continually tighten. This will challenge restaurant owners in attracting and retaining qualified workers. A second threat to the industry is government regulations. Restaurants need to comply with various national, regional and local regulations related to food quality, sanitation and labor rules[3]. Additional regulations may further strain profit margins.

Industry Revenues and Growth

Detailed SWOT Analysis

SWOT analysis:

---

[3] Statista.com

Strengths
Management
  experience.
Strategic plans
Trendy restaurant
  concept
Employee training

Weakness
Startup company.
Untested business
  location.

Opportunities
Community
  involvement
Appeal to a wide
  variety of clientele.
Brand building

Threats
Local competitors
Susceptible to
  economic
  downturn.

Competitive Analysis

(Competitor 1)

(Competitor 1) is located (address). This is about (number) miles from our proposed location. The restaurant offers (menu items). Based on a (Google or Facebook) search, important information was obtained. Previous customers, based on reviews, had mostly (good or bad) reviews. Specifically, a main area discussed was (what was most talked about on Google or Facebook reviews). As a result of the (Google or Facebook) reviews, the restaurant currently has a (number) star rating.

(Competitor 2)

(Competitor 1) is located (address). This is about (number) miles from our proposed location. The restaurant offers (menu items).

Based on a (Google or Facebook) search, important information was obtained. Previous customers, based on reviews, had mostly (good or bad) reviews. Specifically, a main area discussed was (what was most talked about on Google or Facebook reviews). As a result of the (Google or Facebook) reviews, the restaurant currently has a (number) star rating.

(Competitor 3)

(Competitor 1) is located (address). This is about (number) miles from our proposed location. The restaurant offers (menu items). Based on a (Google or Facebook) search, important information was obtained. Previous customers, based on reviews, had mostly (good or bad) reviews. Specifically, a main area discussed was (what was most talked about on Google or Facebook reviews). As a result of the (Google or Facebook) reviews, the restaurant currently has a (number) star rating.

Organization and Management

Management Summary

(Owner name) is the founder and CEO of (restaurant name), which is a (business legal structure: sole proprietor, limited liability restaurant, partnership, corporation). (He or she) has (number) years' experience in the restaurant industry. From this experience, (owner name) has developed specialized critical skills needed to lead and manage this endeavor.

Job Responsibilities

CEO:

- Create and execute all business strategies for growth.
- Align restaurant strategies with mission and vision statement.
- Negotiating contracts with vendors and suppliers.
- Ensure all laws are follow in the restaurant.
- Continually examine the firm's external environment for new opportunities.

Manager:

- Control inventory to ensure optimal levels are achieved.
- Manage day-to-day operations of the restaurant.
- Help servers and cooks during high volume times.
- Interview and hire new employees.
- Assist in the onboarding process for new employees.

Ast. Manager:

- Conduct initial interviews for hiring.
- Floor operations.
- Responsible for taking front of house inventory.
- Opening and closing restaurant.
- Sign off on all side work for front and back of house.

Servers:

- Greet customers.
- Take food and drink orders.
- Deliver food and drinks.
- Ensure quality of visit.
- Collect payment for meal and drinks.

Cooks

- Ensure food tastes and is presented consistently on each and every order.
- Food Preparation.
- Ensure Cleanliness standards.
- Responsible for daily food inventory.
- Sign off on kitchen staff cleaning and side work responsibilities.

Dishwasher

- Collect used dishes from dining and kitchen areas.

- Store clean dishes, glasses and equipment.
- Set up workstations and continually stock before meal prep begins.
- Maintain cleaning supplies.
- Check and adjust washing machines operation temperatures.

Organizational Chart

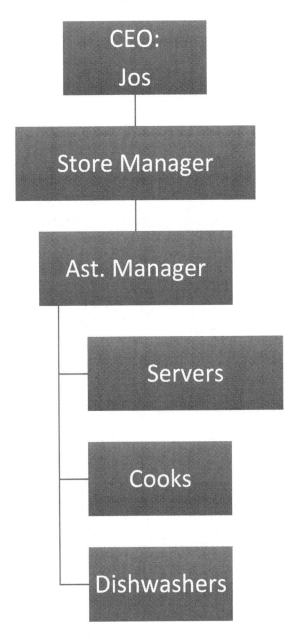

Marketing

Marketing Objectives and Keys to Success

Objectives	Keys to Success
Objective 1.	Key to Success-1
Objective 2.	Key to Success-2
Objective 3.	Key to Success-3
Objective 4.	

Traditional Marketing

Our first traditional marketing channel will include a (discuss your advertising ideas related to mailers, building signs, etc.).

Internet Marketing

The importance of a professionally designed website cannot be understated. To exploit this opportunity, (restaurant name) will create and maintain a website with links to our social media channels. The objective for the strategy is to effectively communicate our menu items that we offer.

Social Media Marketing

(Name of restaurant)'s social media advertising will include Instagram, Twitter, and Facebook. Using a three-channel approach to social media will ensure our message reaches a broad audience, which will include our target market.

Financial Projections

Financial Assumptions

Our financial projections have several assumptions based on research and management's expectation of potential sales and costs.

- All financial projections are based on management and or owner(s) professional expectations of sales and expenses for the foreseeable future.

- In the first 12 months, sales should increase by approximately (percent)% each month. In months 13 to 24, sales growth should slow to approximately (percent)% per month. For years three through five, sales are expected to grow by (percent)%.

- The cost of goods or variable costs are expected to be approximately (percent)% of total sales.

- The initial advertising budget will be $(dollar amount). Advertising is projected to increase by approximately (percent)% per year. This is to ensure maximum utilization of the firm's assets.

- Cost projections were calculated using a common size model. This practice is typical for financial modeling.

- The tax rate was assumed to be (percent)%. Fluctuation in the tax rate will have a direct impact on net profits.

- Initial funding needed is $(dollar amount). An increase/decrease in amount will impact net present value and internal rate of return.

- Starting cash balance needed is $(dollar amount) for working capital.

- Cash account was used to balance assets with liabilities and equity.

Financial Summary

The financial projections are based on market research and empirical examination of the restaurant industry. For the next year, we project revenues of approximately $(dollar amount). The estimated expense costs will be $(dollar amount). After taxes, we estimate a net profit of $(dollar amount). This leads to a profit margin of approximately (percent)%. As our brand continues to grow, second-year progression is anticipated to yield a net income of approximately $(dollar amount). Within five years, net income should exceed $(dollar amount).

Startup Costs

Startup Costs	
Category	**Estimate**
Equity Investment	
Loan	
Initial Build Out	
Working Capital	
Section: Equipment	
Sub Total	
Section: Operations	
Sub Total	

Section: Office Equipment	
Sub Total	
Section: Other	
Sub Total	
Total	

Daily Revenues

Average Daily Sales						
Revenue Generators						
Daily Sales	Num.	Price	Cost	Profit	Total Rev.	Total Cost
Section 1						
Item 1						
Item 2						
Item 3						
Section 2						
Item 1						
Item 2						
Item 3						
				Total		

Labor

Labor				
Employee	Number	Rate	Monthly Hours	Total Pay

Salary				
Manager				
Employees				
			Total	

Monthly Fixed Costs

Monthly Fixed Costs	
Monthly Costs	**Monthly Total**
Rent	
Utilities	
Office Expenses	
Insurance	
Accounting/legal	
Advertising	
Other	
Monthly Total	

Growth Rates

Growth Rates	
Growth Rate Sales 2 & 3	%
Growth Rate Sales 4 & 5	%
Growth Rate Cost of Goods	%
Growth Rate Salary	%
Growth Rate Labor	%
Growth Advertising	%
Growth Office	%
Growth Utility	%
Growth Legal	%
Growth Insurance	%
Growth Other	%

Misc. Information

138

Misc. Information	
Tax Rate	%
Cost of Capital	%

Loan Payment Calculations

Loan Information	
Loan Amount	
Interest Rate	%
Term	
Payment	

Profit and Loss Quarter 1

Pro Forma Income Statement Year 1 Quarter 1				
	Month 1	Month 2	Month 3	Quarter 1
Revenues				
COGS				
Gross Profit				
Expenses				
Salary				
Labor				
Advertising				
Office Expen.				
Rent				
Utilities				
Legal / Account				
Insurance				
Depreciation				
Other				

Total Expenses				
EBIT				
Interest Expense				
EBT				
Taxes				
Net Income				

Profit and Loss Quarter 2

Pro Forma Income Statement Year 1 Quarter 2				
	Month 1	**Month 2**	**Month 3**	**Quarter 1**
Revenues				
COGS				
Gross Profit				
Expenses				
Salary				
Labor				
Advertising				
Office Expen.				
Rent				
Utilities				
Legal / Account				
Insurance				
Depreciation				
Other				
Total Expenses				

EBIT				
Interest Expense				
EBT				
Taxes				
Net Income				

Profit and Loss Quarter 3

Pro Forma Income Statement Year 1 Quarter 3				
	Month 1	Month 2	Month 3	Quarter 1
Revenues				
COGS				
Gross Profit				
Expenses				
Salary				
Labor				
Advertising				
Office Expen.				
Rent				
Utilities				
Legal / Account				
Insurance				
Depreciation				
Other				
Total Expenses				
EBIT				
Interest Expense				

EBT			
Taxes			
Net Income			

Profit and Loss Quarter 4

Pro Forma Income Statement Year 1 Quarter 4			
	Month 1	Month 2	Month 3	Quarter 1
Revenues			
COGS			
Gross Profit			
Expenses			
Salary			
Labor			
Advertising			
Office Expen.			
Rent			
Utilities			
Legal / Account			
Insurance			
Depreciation			
Other			
Total Expenses			
EBIT			
Interest Expense			
EBT			
Taxes			
Net Income			

Income Statement

Pro Forma Income Statement Year 1 Quarter 1				
	Year 1	Year 2	Year 3	Year 4
Revenues				
COGS				
Gross Profit				
Expenses				
Salary				
Labor				
Advertising				
Office Expen.				
Rent				
Utilities				
Legal / Account				
Insurance				
Depreciation				
Other				
Total Expenses				
EBIT				
Interest Expense				
EBT				
Taxes				
Net Income				

Balance Sheet

Balance Sheet - Pro Forma					
Assets	Year 1	Year 2	Year 3	Year 4	Year 5
Cash					
Accts Receiv.					
Invent.					
Total Curr. Assets					
PP&E					
Less Deprec.					
Net PP&E					
Total Assets					

Balance Sheet - Pro Forma					
Liabilities	Year 1	Year 2	Year 3	Year 4	Year 5
Accounts Pay					
Notes Payable					
Accruals					
Total Current Liab.					
Loans					
Total Liab.					
Common Stock					
Retained Earnings					
Total Com. Equity					
Total Liab & Equity					

Financial Ratios

Financial Ratios					
	Year 1	Year 2	Year 3	Year 4	Year 5
Return on Equity					
Return on Asset					
Current Ratio					
Profit Margin					
Net Present Value					
IRR					

Funding Request

To start operations, funding of $(dollar amount) in debt or equity from a bank or investor is required. Debt funding is expected to have a term of (number) to (number) years with an interest rate between (percent)% to (percent)%. Principle and interest payments will be made monthly, using profits from the business. For investors, a negotiated percentage of ownership in the restaurant will be offered. In addition, investors will be compensated through (monthly, quarter, semi-annually) dividend payments from business cash flows.

Received funds will be used as follows:

Startup Costs	
Category	Estimate
Equity Investment	
Loan	
Initial Build Out	
Working Capital	
Section: Equipment	
Sub Total	
Section: Operations	
Sub Total	
Section: Office Equipment	

Sub Total	
Section: Other	
Sub Total	
Total	

64904987R00090